*For Bill —
fellow traveler.
Cheers —*

Crossroads

by
Grace Butcher

*Grace Butcher
2-2-19*

Selected Columns
from *Rider* 1979-1985
and
articles from *Sports Illustrated*
and *Whatever It Takes*

Acknowledgements

Front cover, center photo by Kathy Briggs.

Front cover, bottom photo by Darlene Fritz.

Other photos from author's scrapbooks. Photographers unknown.

"Where the Poems Come From Now that I Ride a Motorcycle"
and "On Motorcycles through Amish Country"
from *Before I Go Out on the Road,*
Cleveland State University Poetry Center, 1979, 1992.

"Cycle Song" from *Rumors of Ecstasy...Rumors of Death,*
Ashland Poetry Press 1971, Barnwood Press 1981.

All columns from *Rider*, 1979-1985.

"So Much Depends on a Red Tent"
from *Sports Illustrated*, February 3, 1975.

"Q: Why do you race? A: Because my name comes apart"
from *Whatever It Takes: Women on Women's Sport.*
Joli Sandoz and Joby Winans, editors.
Farrar, Strauss and Giroux 1999.

Book design by Ken Duncan

Copyright ©2007 by Grace Butcher

ISBN 978-0-9786550-1-3

Table of Contents

Introduction 5
Where the Poems Come from Now that I Ride a Motorcycle 7
What Goes Up... 7
For These Reasons 10
Grading Papers, Changing the Oil 12
Why Didn't I...? 15
The Joys of Touring Alone 17
On the Lonely Road 20
Just Puttering Along 22
The Errand-Running Machine 24
Visiting the Past 26
Secret Love 30
Better Off at Home 33
New Perceptions 36
On Motorcycles Through Amish Country 38
Paranoia 40
Daydreaming 42
All Alone 44
Anticipation 46
With a Little Help 50
Saved by Instinct 52
More Odds and Ends 54
Synchronicity 56
Lessons Learned 59
Visions of a First Rally 61
Underneath The Arches 63
Elixir for an Octogenarian 66
Friendly Encounters 68
Sounds to Sleep and Wake by 70
Moods 73
First Ride 75
Cycle Song 77
Almost Never 78
Miles of Smiles 81
Contributions to Safe Riding 83
Gripes 85
Fast, Faster, Fastest 87
European Gleanings 89
Sense Impressions 92

Tunnel Vision	95
Pride Goeth	96
All My Worldly Goods	99
On the Lonely Road	102
Following Instincts	104
So Many Dreams to Choose From	106
How to Ride in the Alps (or not)	108
A Hole in Time	110
The Other Road	113
The Secret Life	115
So Much Depends upon a Red Tent	118
Q: Why do you want to race? A: Because my name comes apart	129

Riding strange bikes over strange roads.

Introduction

In 1973, a serious foot problem was preventing me from training for track competition after many years on the national scene. Although it was fixed by surgery a couple of years later, then I felt it to be an identity crisis of major proportion: if I'm not a runner, who will I be? Never mind that I was a college professor and a writer; these seemed just something I did. Being a runner — that was the real me.

But about that time, along came a handsome young man on a motorcycle who confidently assumed I'd want to have my own bike soon. And I did. And then I went to watch another — yes — handsome young man race motocross, and after growing up riding horses, I thought, "I could do that!" And I did. The fact that I was 39 when I started street riding and 40 when I started racing seemed irrelevant. As the old Zen saying has it, "When the pupil is ready, the teacher will appear."

Early in 1979, as I read another keenly-awaited issue of *Rider* magazine, which I'd subscribed to soon after I started riding, a notice in the back caught my eye: "DO YOU RIDE AND WRITE?" They were looking for a women's editor! Ride and write? I'd always written, kept journals since age 14, published several books of poetry, some sports articles, and I'd just written one of the books for a series called *Women in Sports,* on women who raced motorcycles. Writing a column for *Rider* seemed the perfect combination of my two passions. I put together a pile of credentials, sent them off to *Rider's* offices in California, and waited.

Several months passed. Oh well, I thought. And then came the phone call. That was one of the most exciting moments of my writerly life! And for six years I wrote the column every month, along with a few feature articles and write-ups of our women's road test trips. I believe *Rider* was the first magazine — maybe the only one — to sometimes use all women for weekend test rides, giving a small group of us brand new bikes and sending us out to ride hard, swap and compare bikes, experience life on the road from a different perspective. Those trips resulted in not only invaluable experience riding strange bikes over strange roads, but in some long-lasting friendships as well.

So from 1979 to 1985 I wrote the columns that make up the better part of this book.

When I found myself re-dedicating most of my time to training for Masters track (age group competition for older athletes), and riding less, it felt like time to "retire" from my very rewarding relationship with the good folks at *Rider* and focus on running again. I am very grateful for those six years with the magazine. That time period had a sort of dreamlike, surreal quality to it, especially when they flew me out to California for the road test trips. I might never have otherwise seen the giant sequoias, Yosemite, the California coast road. I'm grateful, too, for my twenty years of riding.

A few years after retiring from teaching at Kent State University Geauga Campus, and while traveling a great deal, I gave my beloved BMW, my 1975 R90/6, to my son in New Hampshire. I couldn't stand seeing it sitting in my garage with cobwebs on it, and now he rides it to work, my daughter-in-law rides it, and maybe someday my grandson and granddaughter will ride it as well.

I think if I have a philosophy of life, it's to discover and fulfill our potential. That goes for man/woman or machine. I think my bike and I are both doing what we were meant to do.

Where the Poems Come from Now that I Ride a Motorcycle

They don't come from the sun
so much anymore —
or not the sun alone
but from the glint of sun
on chrome.

And not so much
from the dark roads
as from the unrolling
of the roads with a sound
like wind.

And sometimes now from
the way the quiet stars
blow back behind me
and I have no thought at all
till later.

I notice how everything is changing;
nothing comes from where it used to.
I make decisions at crossroads
I have never seen before.
So does the wind.

The directions we are heading
have not yet even been named.

from *Before I Go Out on the Road*
Cleveland State University Poetry Center 1979

What Goes Up...

    After it was all over, I realized I would have had trouble getting my 125 dirt bike up that hill, let alone my full-dress 900 BMW. What on earth had I been thinking? Well, what I'd been thinking was two things. One, I'd never yet camped without my bike securely chained to something an arm's length away; and two, I must really be a pretty hot-shot rider now because I'd won a fourth place trophy in motocross a few weeks ago, hadn't I?

And here I was, first day out on my second major tour, alone, traveling to North Carolina to visit my son and on to Florida to see my aunt. Oh brave and wonderful me! After about 10 hours on the road, I'd been glad to find that state park in West Virginia and pick out a pretty campsite on top of a hill. Why couldn't I have been content to leave the bike just a few yards down below in the little gravel parking area?

First I walked the hill like any good motocrosser would walk the course, muttering, "Let's see now ... if I go up to here and turn here and then go up there ... OK." In my head it all looked pretty good. In the real world the problems started in the first 10 yards when the front wheel disappeared into a grassy rut the great motocrosser hadn't even noticed. Get off the bike, pull, haul, push, swear, sweat, tremble. Whew! There, I'm out. Steer around the rut this time, dummy, and now the final run to the top. Just straight up this little slope here ...

I'd never thought about the wet grass. Halfway up the rear wheel started spinning. I put both feet down, paddling as hard as I could, trying to throttle and brake at the same time so as not to slide down while I'm trying to go up. What to do! My feet kept slipping on the grass and the bike acting as if it was tired of all this hill climbing and wanting to lie down. Looking rather wildly around I saw a guy some distance away setting up a tent. "Hey, can you help me?" I shouted, trying to sound as calm and sophisticated as possible, as if being stuck halfway up a slippery hill in West Virginia on a rather large motorcycle was, of course, just part of my normal, everyday routine.

He ran over and got behind the bike, pushing as hard as he could, his feet slipping on the wet grass too. Finally we made it to the top, and I thanked him as he walked away. Drenched with sweat inside my touring leathers, and shaking slightly, I sat on my bike at the top of that hill and contemplated my fate: BMWs, when ridden by small, slender women — even by small, slender, athletic women who race motocross do not belong on the top of Mt. Everest. Hopefully I looked at the sky to see if maybe a helicopter pilot had heard of my plight and come to airlift me and my bike back down to the little parking area. None in sight. What goes up must come down. I prepared to do it then and there, knowing I'd have trouble sleeping just thinking about it.

No point in trying to make those turns on the way down; might as well go straight down slowly and hope for the best. But minutes went by while I sat immobilized by anxiety, hoping anyone who saw me would think I was merely sitting there on my great white bike, posed majestically on top of the hill, watching the sunset: the ultimate touring rider, silhouetted against the sky, inseparable from her faithful motorcycle. (I'd always wondered how a sky diver felt, poised in the airplane door for that first jump.)

Finally I started down. And I realized immediately that the word "slowly" had been only wishful thinking. Using the brakes on the wet grass was a mistake; I started to go sideways, straightened it up, and found myself hurtling down the hill towards the little gravel parking lot. No brakes there either, not in that gravel — I overshot the lot and went plunging down over the next hillside right for a bunch of trees and picnic tables. Only thing to do was lay it down, and that I did, slithering to a halt just short of being crammed under the nearest table.

From back on the hill a distance away, the very same man who'd helped push me *up* only minutes before came running to see if I was all right. "Oh boy," I said to myself, wiggling out from under the bike as casually as possible. I could imagine what he was thinking: "What in the world is this idiot woman *doing* out here alone with this motorcycle?" (Actually I'd begun to wonder the same thing myself.) Another astonished spectator ran over, and the three of us laboriously pushed the bike back up the wet hillside. I thanked them calmly, determined to maintain even unto death my facade of sophisticated traveler (hadn't I read somewhere that you were *supposed* to practice laying it down just in case you even had to?). Ignoring their exchange of incredulous glances as they walked away, I parked the unscathed bike where I should have left it in the first place, parked my severely damaged ego under a tree outside my tent. and sat brooding, pondering what I had learned.

Pride goeth before a fall. It never seems to fail. Every time I reach the point where I start feeling a little cocky, something happens to put me down, sometimes quite literally. Slowly I've learned to try not to get myself into situations with the bike where either my small size or a lack of common sense would get me in trouble or force me to ask for help. Most women who ride seem to feel that they come under pretty close scrutiny, and having to ask for help can be embarrassing, especially to the self-conscious new rider. Better not to get into the situation at all, if possible. I remember a motel parking lot in Maine, newly and deeply graveled ... but that's another story.

Learning to recognize the situation in advance takes time and experience for all riders. And why is it that all those Mt. Everests in everybody's cycling lives seem so funny afterwards? I'll bet I could compile a book of all our touring ticklers and camping comedies called something like ... *Places I Have Been (And Couldn't Get Out Of).* The first story would start out like this: "I *knew* I shouldn't have tried to take my Harley Electra Glide on that white-water canoeing trip, but. ... "

Rider November 1979

For These Reasons

What stays in my mind from when I was first learning to ride is that everything was golden. It was October of 1973 and I had my first motorcycle, a GT250 Suzuki.

Clumsy, filled with anxiety, amazed at my own courage, and as carefully as I could, I rode 100 miles alone each of the first three days I ever rode. No fairing, no windshield. The wind seemed awesome, and I was incredibly tired at the end of each day's ride. But I wanted to learn to be a better rider *(good* wasn't even a word I allowed myself yet), and it seemed to me then that 100 miles a day was the best way to get better. And though I remember the tension and fatigue and determination, it's the incredible golden glow of October in Ohio that I remember most.

Northeastern Ohio is a little like New England with its hills and farms and curving, climbing, country roads. With that most curious and uniquely human sense of awareness, I was both participant and observer, or as Thoreau wrote in *Walden,* we are like spectators at our own events. Along that narrow, shaded road by the river — how could such golden trees make such dark shadows? I felt to be both rider and watcher, part of my awareness functioning as if I were high above the scene watching myself ride down those quiet gray and black and bright ribbons of road.

To be out there alone with the meadows curving around me like emerald oceans, the sky an empty, blazing, brilliant blue, and those endless miles of golden trees gilding the hills, and the hills like piles of golden coins — the intensity of it was unreal. And most dream-like of all, I was riding my first very own motorcycle.

And on into the gradual grays and browns of November, shivering and edgy in the dank winds, wrapping my legs around the warm body of my bike, riding until drops of cold rain hit my new windshield breaking the landscape into blurred images, and the gloom settled heavily over the fading afternoon and I turned, still shivering, for home.

And those rare, clear, snowless days in winter when salt gleamed on the bare roads like broken glass, and the sharp edges of the January air cut my face with endless invisible blades, and the motorists stared from their warm and isolated cubicles as if I were crazy. Maybe I was.

But then there was spring with its filmy green lace over everything like green smoke on the bare hills. Twilight dropped me into a sudden, dark, and starry cold, but daytime turned my leather jacket warm in the sun across my shoulders, and I luxuriated in it like a lazy beast just awakening.

Summer seemed a brilliant shimmering, blue and green and all colors, filling the air with the sweet bright smell of hot clover, or layers of perfumed lilac drifting through the black velvet midnight, and when I'd look up, the stars were silver streaks through the warm darkness.

I've ridden through six turnings of the seasons now, and I can walk into my garage and never notice my car, never think about it even when I get into it. But every single time I open the garage door and walk into the dim interior, my eyes go at once to my bike gleaming there back against the wall, chained like a wild animal, looming big and white and seeming to glow in the dimness with some kind of light of its own. On days I do not ride it, I touch it, caress it as I walk by.

Six years. Sixty years. I hope it will always be like this with these machines, these creatures that we love so, that we feed and groom and unchain so they may take us, heroically astride, into yet another adventure. A trip to the post office in the car is just an errand, but I am excited before I even step out of the house when I am going on the bike. Every single time.

I've never written poems about my car. When I drive it, no heads turn as I go by, no little children wave with longing in their eyes. My car is merely a temporary shell for the soft, peculiar animal inside. No one is interested, not even me. But astride my bike I am a centaur reincarnated from mythology into the midst of our startling technology. My hooves are wheels, my mane is my own hair, my body an exotic blending of muscle and machinery.

"Why in the world do you want to ride a motorcycle?" people always ask me. I just smile.

Rider December 1979

Grading Papers, Changing the Oil

Recently a new student stuck his head into my office "I hear you ride," he said. I acknowledged that was true, waving at the motocross trophy blatantly displayed on my desk and the huge BMW poster on the wall. "Well, I've got this Norton and it's just not running right. I was wondering if you'd ride it for me and see what's wrong with it."

A strange mixture of feelings ran through me at that moment. A man was asking me, a woman, to determine what the problem was with his motorcycle. "It's got this bad vibration over 4,000 rpm, he continued. I nodded my head non-committally as silently, to myself, I was answering him, "It's a Norton, oh naive one. It's going to vibrate at anything over one rpm." But then I realized that wasn't fair — sort of like saying that all Italians are passionate or that all redheads have hot tempers. Better to wait and see.

At the same time I had to suppress a smile. He seemed to be assuming that because I both rode a motorcycle and was a college professor, of course I would know what was wrong with anybody's bike, just like I'd know what was wrong with anybody's composition: "Hmm, let's see (tinker, tinker). This bike seems to have a particple dangling from its crankcase. And, oh yes, your infinitive is split here — see — right by the air filter housing? Timing's a little off in your verb tenses too, but we'll take care of that. Hand me that feeler gauge, would ya? It's right there next to my red pencil."

...because I both rode a motorcycle and was a college professor, of course I would know what was wrong with anybody's bike...

And still at the same time two other reactions were going on. (Isn't it amazing how many thoughts can seem to occur simultaneously in the human mind?) One of my many voices was saying to me in a rather cynical tone, "Come on, Grace. You're not going to know what's wrong with his bike." And right on top of that voice, another me was saying with great interest, "But listen, you just might figure it out."

Growing up female in our culture can do some peculiar things to us. We're not supposed to know how to handle math, money, or machinery. And even now when I set out alone to deal with something mechanical on any of my bikes, there's that little twinge of anxiety. Fear of the unknown.

But I had to start somewhere, and my dirt bike didn't seem to mind. "Watch, this is how you take off the chain to clean it, and you have to do it after every race," a motocross friend had begun. And I watched intently the friend who'd taught me to ride do several tuneups on my BMW while he explained every move. But I seem to learn tactilely, not visually; I have to feel with my hands how something is done. What does "snug" mean when you're setting the points? "Here, let me feel how the gauge is supposed to be." I feel metal sliding tightly against metal, the thin, flexible blade of the gauge against the tiny round smoothness of the new points. "Oh, I see." (Or rather, I feel.)

I remember one time on my way to school when the whole electrical system just quit. And this time I knew what to look at first, discovering the positive contact for the battery cable corroded almost away and being able to make a temporary contact with the small stub remaining. Shame, shame on me for neglecting to clean that. (But it went so fast! The positive post had been leaking.) The reason I knew what to look for was that on an early tour of mine, I'd once been stranded in a stranger's yard somewhere in the Kentucky mountains with a bike that wouldn't start, and because he'd happened to be a biker and looked first thing at the battery and found the terminals an evil looking mess of seething green corrosion, I eventually learned about keeping a battery clean, even if it did take me two lessons instead of one.

And when the carburetors on my road race bike needed to be disassembled and cleaned after racing in the rain and there was nobody around to help me and it had to be done before the next race, in desperation I took them apart myself and cleaned them. And put them back together! That was one of the triumphant moments of my life. I stood there in the hot sun in my driveway, revving the engine, hearing that sharp, clear, rackety two-stroke sound, envisioning the shiny golden slides lifting and dropping smoothly inside their miniature black towers. I smiled and smiled.

I'm still very frustrated by all I don't know about working on bikes. Yet when I think of what I knew a few years ago — nothing — I feel more patient. There's an enormous gratification in being female, sitting on the floor in my garage with my hands dirty, tools and parts spread out around me, and having some non-mechanical male acquaintance drop in. "Wow, really looks like you know what you're doing," he might say. I give a modest shrug, hoping that my simple oil change will look to him like at least a complete engine overhaul. "Well, I try."

And that's the whole point: trying. Maybe I *will* know what's wrong with that guy's Norton when I ride it. And if I don't, I'll for sure know what's wrong with his composition the first time he writes one. Feeler gauge, red pencil — it's all kind of the same thing: just tryin' to get the bugs out.

Rider January 1980

Along the Cabot Trail in Nova Scotia

Why Didn't I...?

I've often thought that the saddest words in the English language must be "if only:" "If only I'd done this ... if only I'd said that .... " And feeling this way, I try to live my life so as to have as few "if onlys" as possible. Yet they *will* crop up, it seems. A kaleidoscopic array of scenes and events swirls through my thoughts as I remember little bits and pieces from tours. Among all the wonderful experiences they seem to hover like vague ghosts haunting my memory. None of them were important, probably. None of them would have changed my life any to speak of, probably. And yet ....

I still see that road along the river in Quebec, the river with its serpentine curves lazily silver in the afternoon sun. I was heading more or less home on my first tour, alone through New England and Canada, and had made a "wrong" turn, east instead of west on Route 1. And yet I had all summer, if I wanted. I could have continued along on that beautiful road with white birches lining the river until I'd arrived somewhere. But no, I turned around after 10 miles or so, realizing that I wasn't headed home. What difference did it make, really — an extra day on the road, an extra hundred miles or two? And now that river and the road beside it still gleam like pewter in the late sun, stretching away into an unknown afternoon more beautiful in my mind than it might ever have been But I'll never know.

And on Route 7 in Vermont one day, one trip, I passed through a tiny settlement tucked away in the hills and pines of that lovely state, and suddenly there was a little motorcycle shop with a BMW parked in front of it and a couple of guys standing beside it They waved and smiled as I rode past, and I waved back Something about the scene made me want to turn around and go back, just to say hello and talk a bit The sun through the trees, the tiny shop speckled with light and shadow, the familiar motorcycle, the pleasant looking men, the friendly wave I felt a surge of warmth, an eagerness to talk to someone; I'd been alone for quite a while. But there it was, another old hangup: Nice girls don't stop and talk to strange men. "Turn around, turn around. Go back and say hello," I kept saying to myself as the yards and then miles spun out irretrievably behind me. And that scene too remains a frozen tableau in my mind: the scent of pine, the warm sun, the little shop, the friendly wave, and the hello I did not say.

And photos left untaken. The great silver cloud of sea gulls that rose and fell, rose and fell behind the tractor and plow in that field in — was it Nova Scotia? — wheeling and swooping in the sun, the gleam of their white wings brilliant against the dark, newly-turned earth. I didn't stop. When I did finally turn around and go back after a mile or two, the birds were gone, the tractor was gone, and only an ordinary field remained.

Or the stunning, brilliant red covered bridge down in southern Ohio on my way to Ohio University in Athens to read poetry. The poetry was there along the road, the bridge amazing in its unexpected coat of scarlet, standing out even among the flaming maples of that Ohio autumn. Why didn't I stop?

Sometimes it was the campsites I did not stop at that I remember more than the ones I did. Along the Cabot Trail in Nova Scotia where I'd ridden for nearly two hours that June morning with hardly another vehicle on the roads, I felt as if someone had given me the whole Highlands National Park for a gift: "Here, have it all to yourself; this is for you!" And along the way was the most beautiful little campsite, nestled down in a cup-like valley in those beautiful mountains. I can still see it; it looked like an illustration from a fairy-tale book, with a crystal lake (and enchanted fish, no doubt) and the blue-green mountains all around. But it was only noon; I couldn't stop then.

I couldn't stop then? Why couldn't I?

What is this sense of urgency that we all feel sometimes on the road, that "gotta keep going" feeling? I had time for that cup of coffee a pleasant couple offered me one morning at a campsite somewhere up in Michigan on the shore of Lake Huron. What difference did that extra 20 minutes make? "No thanks, I've got to be going." Not true. I didn't have to be going. But the road was pulling me out there with an almost tangible force; the intensity I feel about getting back on the road is almost distressing at times. What's my hurry? I have to work at relaxing. I have to plan not to plan. And I have to learn to listen to that little voice that says, "Whoa. Slow down. Stop. Take the photo, right now. Talk to those people. Have that cup of coffee." Maybe it was being alone that caused me to keep going, keep busy, keep riding. I'm not brooding on "The Road Not Taken," to steal a title from Robert Frost. The past is past. But I want to remember these things I didn't do, to remind me to do them, whatever they are, next time.

Rider March 1980

The Joys of Touring Alone

The joys of touring with a friend are obvious, and the sharing of memories is something we all enjoy. "Hey, remember when you got your seventeenth flat tire on the Alcan Highway and I had to grab your arm to keep you from fixin' it with your hatchet?" And that long wait under the bridge in the rain and the dark and the cold? It goes a lot faster if there's a friend to talk to: "Oh yeah, we'll find a campsite soon. Sure, sure we will. If we'd stopped at that motel two hours ago the way I wanted .... "

Well, actually there always seem to be more good memories than bad from trips together assuming you both get to where you were going alive and in one piece. Traveling together has its own special rewards. But what about touring alone? Most people don't think anything of jumping into a car or onto a plane alone for a long business trip or a visit to Aunt Dorothy. But let it be known that you plan to take a long motorcycle tour alone, and immediately you're in a room full of echoes: "Alone? You're going alone? Are you crazy?"

What would the reasons be for a woman (or a man, for that matter) to actually *want* to tour alone? I can share with you some of my own reasons for wanting — maybe even needing — to take some long, leisurely, two- to three-week trips by myself. And I'm pretty sure that a lot of you already know or will soon find out these reasons for yourselves.

First, our lives often seem to have those high points — plateaus of one kind or another — from which we look around and realize that we are ready for some sort of adventure. The timing seems right for a declaration of independence, with small letters but big meaning. A trip alone is a major statement about what kind of person we are, or want to be.

So much of our life is spent interacting with others that we may finally say to ourselves, "I am this way with Joe and that way with Susie, but what am I like with just myself for company?" I've always been puzzled by the idea of going away "to find" oneself. That notion reminds me of a Zen saying, "Oh foolish people, you run around carrying torches, looking for fire!" And as a wonderful line in a poem by David Wagoner puts it, we can never really be lost, for "Wherever you are is called Here." Whatever it is we are, is always with us, but we are seldom alone to experience it. For those of us who ride, what better way to get in touch with our Solo Self (otherwise known as the Soul, maybe?) than by being alone out on the road. I had an intense curiosity to see how I would be away from the secure and comforting routine of home life, unable to prepare for what was around the next bend, not knowing where I'd sleep till I got there, thinking and reacting completely on my own.

Probably growing up an only child and living in the country most of my life had a great deal to do with my feeling that doing things alone was the normal state of affairs. And having my own way most of the time was, I confess, a most enjoyable situation. And being alone on the road is surely one way to have your own way. Oh, a chuckhole might decide to bend a rim for you or a rainstorm to put you under that bridge. But where you turn, stop, stay. eat, camp — these are all your decisions.

For a woman, particularly, a sense of independence is one of the headiest feelings imaginable. And the accompanying feelings of delight and adventure I've experienced on a trip alone are often getting on towards ecstatic, especially the almost unbearable excitement of starting out: Riding down the driveway in my touring leathers, my pack on behind and 2,000 miles of road ahead "Imagine doing such a thing!" I say to myself proudly and incredulously, feeling as if I'm the star in a movie that is portraying the life of an unbelievably adventurous woman.

And for a woman, the ego rewards of touring alone can be absolutely stunning. A man alone on a bike and obviously touring is a fairly commonplace scene, while a woman doing the same thing is still regarded with amazement. The friendliness and curiosity of most people have always delighted me. Seldom have I been completely ignored in a campsite; someone often invites me to join a family circle around the campfire or offers a cup of coffee or a hobo pie (especially when I most want to be alone to write, it seems). Restaurant parking lots often produce a number of friendly conversations as do rest areas and scenic lookout spots. I've found that a pleasant nod and a "hello" on my part will almost always break through another tourist's blank stare — blank mainly, I suspect, because of being at a loss for words. How does one address this apparition — a leather-clad female touring rider, alone!

In spite of confrontations with an amicable public, most of the time is spent. as I would wish, alone. How often are we given these hours of clear access to the insides of our heads? The opportunity to deal with an incredible variety of situations completely on our own? To be sure, there are anxieties inherent in such a trip, but that's another column. For now, let's just say that a solo tour, especially that very first one, will probably be one of the greatest memories any rider can have.

Rider April 1980

On the Lonely Road

I had dreamed of finding such a place. The view from the campsite high on a hill in Nova Scotia was stunning. Far below, the quiet ocean lay smooth and golden in the late afternoon sun, curving into a deserted crescent beach of reddish sand After slowly, peacefully setting up camp, I'd ridden back down the road a few miles to eat in a superb restaurant that used to be a schooner, and now I was back, full of lobster, sitting alone watching the ocean turn from sunset gold to silver gray to starlit black. Tomorrow, I thought eagerly, I would ride the Cabot Trail around the tip of Nova Scotia, my glorious goal after 1,800 miles of riding. Then as I sat there, to my astonishment something very unusual happened. I felt lonely.

I don't know — maybe it was the incredible scenery and no one to share it with, although that hadn't bothered me on any of my other trips. Maybe it was because tomorrow I'd ride a loop through the Highlands National Park that would turn me around, head me towards home, and the word "home" caused a sudden contraction just a little southwest of my heart. Or maybe it was because whatever I've had to prove to myself on my other trips alone had already been proven.

And as if to prolong my somber mood, sleep seemed to have been delayed somewhere along the line. It didn't show up for the longest time, and when it did arrive, it was only half-hearted and didn't want to stay. So all night long I listened to the wind walking strangely in the grass around my tent. I don't know how many times I unzipped the tent to look around and see who was there No one.

This was not a typical experience, for usually I loved being alone on the road, in restaurants, in campsites, talking to people occasionally but for the most part feeling sort of mysteriously folded in upon myself, being quiet, writing in my journal, focusing on my moods. Usually a kind of joy pervaded my days and nights alone; being alone itself seemed to be the cause. But sometimes, in addition to loneliness, another dark dimension would intrude: fear.

Once in the hills of southern Ohio, two guys in a pickup truck played pass-me games, drinking beer and tossing the cans out along the roadside. They'd pull over up ahead, watch me go by, sit there long enough to be out of sight in my rearview mirrors. Then there they'd be again, framed in those little shivering silver circles on my handlebars, the images growing larger while my heart thumped wildly and I wondered what would happen, what to do. And then the game was over; they were gone as suddenly as they had appeared.

And the man in the yellow Mustang who followed me for miles through the mountains of eastern Kentucky, refusing to pass, slowing down when I slowed down, speeding up when I did. I'd looked at the map and thought that road would make a nice shortcut through that corner of Kentucky. Instead it corkscrewed ominously back and back upon itself, heading up and down, up and down, but never seeming to go anywhere. Nothing remotely resembled a safe place to pull off and be among people, and it was getting on towards evening. The mountain landscape seemed more and more desolate. Why had I ever taken this road? All afternoon I'd been sandwiched between coal trucks hurtling down hills behind me, creeping up the hills in front of me. In places the road had fallen away from the mountain leaving a one-lane dirt path under repair. And now this car behind me for an hour.

Suddenly I saw a little weatherbeaten store with a pleasant looking man sitting in front of it, and impulsively I whipped over and pulled in. The car went on by. I told the young man I thought I was being followed, and as I talked, the yellow Mustang came back past, slowed, and kept on going. "You just go on," the young man said kindly. "I'll keep watch, and if that guy comes back again, I'll get in my car and follow him just to be sure he doesn't bother you. But he won't catch up to you now, once you get 10 minutes ahead. You'll be OK." And an hour up the road a miraculous couple appeared, sitting on a motorcycle at an ice cream place in a little mining town They invited me home, gave me their absent daughter's bedroom and a great breakfast the next morning, instructed me to "foller this-here road till y'all get to that there road and purty soon, why you'll be somewhere afore you know it!" And I was.

And the long steel grate bridges, and the sudden violent thunderstorms with the rain sweeping sideways and the lightning crackling down all around and deep ditches and narrow berms and no place to pull over. And the half dozen rowdy, obscene drunks who pulled in, in the middle of the night, and camped next to me in a relatively deserted state park. Seeing my motorcycle parked nearby, they wouldn't know I was a woman alone, I figured, but I lay sleepless.

So I've been scared a few times on trips alone. And lonely once or twice. (And guilty of occasional understatement.) But the fear always passes and never seems so bad in the retelling. And by the same token, the joy passes too and blends into sorrow which turns again into delight, and so on. It's this constant swirl of emotion that gives a trip alone an intensity that somehow overshadows the anxiety. It's as if when I ride alone, my body is a harp that the wind plays on, touching every string, every nerve-ending. The music is frightening sometimes, but haunting. I always seem to want to hear it again.

Rider May 1980

Just Puttering Along

I remember one day last fall — a gorgeous late September afternoon — when I'd ridden the three miles into town to get my mail and do some errands. I had to get right back, for my desk was piled high with student compositions: about 10 hours' worth of papers to grade. And the lawn had to be mowed, and the house put into some kind of order, and something had to be read for class the next day. Probably half a dozen other chores were jumping up and down on my list of things to do. "I've got to get back," I was muttering to myself as I left the post office That musky, alluring smell of late fall was in the air as I reluctantly turned towards my house, and I rode along feeling very sorry for myself.

I hadn't been so depressed in a long time. Somehow or other I'd always seemed to find time to "just ride" when I was first learning. And now here I was, trapped by my conscience, shoulders slumped in gloom, heading back home on this beautiful day when I wanted so badly to ride.

But as I approached my driveway, my motorcycle started behaving strangely. It kept veering towards the center line when I tried to turn it. Dumbfounded. I struggled with it, but to no avail. It was running away from home and taking me with it! I was a helpless victim of circumstance. Who could have predicted such a thing?

"Listen," I pleaded with it. "I've got to get those papers graded. My students .... "

"Putter, putter, putter," it answered (BMW talk).

"Yes, I know," I said, "but look. I won't mow the lawn; I'll just grade the papers if you'll only take me back. OK?"

"Hmmmmmm," it sang, a little happy tune all its own

By then we were a mile or more down the road. The bike seemed to be going very fast; there was just no holding it. "Well. ..." I sighed, beginning to resign myself to the fact that I was being held prisoner by an incredibly handsome motorcycle that seemed hell bent on delivering me to some unknown destination out toward the horizon of this magnificent, multi-colored autumn afternoon.

"Look," I addressed my abductor. "I give up. I'm not going to try to escape. Why don't you Just slow down a little bit, and we can enjoy the scenery?" (which did seem to be going by in kind of a red-orange blur).

Well, by then the bike seemed amenable to suggestion. Eighty in a 45 zone, even out in the country, did seem a bit much to both of us. We were safely out of the magnetic force field of my house; my things-to-do list was a memory fading as rapidly as my last twinges of guilt, and I settled in to enjoy my captivity and to shake my head at what things had come to, that my bike had to run away with me like this.

All that work would wait, but this afternoon would never come again. I was so busy being busy these days that my bike seemed to become a part of all that: ride to school, teach my classes, ride home, ride to get the mail. ride to get some groceries, ride home What had happened to those days of just riding? Why did I always seem to have to have somewhere to get to? The question, "Where shall we go?" often bothered me when I rode with a friend sometimes on weekends. Why did we have to have a place to go? Couldn't we just ride and see where we ended up?

Sometimes we would deliberately turn onto roads we'd never ridden before, just to see what was down there And sooner or later there'd always be that little restaurant with the good cup of coffee and piece of pie, wherever we were.

So on this day I just puttered along, taking any old road, growing happier and happier as the miles went by. Psychologists believe that people who are kidnapped and held hostage often seem to fall in love with their kidnappers. Yes, I confess. That's what happened to me. And do you know where we ended up? At a cheese factory where I bought — are you ready for this? — some chocolate cheese. And a little way up the road was a stream to sit by and a tree to lean against while I ate it. I didn't even know there was such a thing as chocolate cheese. But I did know that I would try not to let busy-ness take over my life again the way it had there for a while. "Just riding." It's one of those things that I never want to forget how to do.

Rider June 1980

The Errand-Running Machine

There's something to be said, all right, for the long tour, the long commute in all sorts of weather. And what's usually said is something that could, just maybe, be mistaken for a little teeny tiny bit of bragging. "Yep, we rode 7,000 miles on that trip. Out a whole month" Or, "It's 87 miles to work, one way, and I ride every day come hell or high water — and say, let me tell you about that last high water. It was clear up to my ...."

I understand all that. There's something really impressive about sheer mileage through heat of day and dark of night. I see there's even a 1,000-miles-in-one-day club advertised. Drawn to endurance activities as I always have been, I feel the attraction of just going and going and going. The current popularity of marathon running seems to serve as evidence that the farther we go, the better we feel about ourselves, the prouder we are. Maybe I'll look into reasons for that in a future column, but this time I'd like to speak to the other side of that issue: the great delight I feel on days when I have a dozen errands to do, all within a five-mile radius, and am on and off the bike more times than I can count.

It would be so much easier just to leave my shorts and T-shirt and sandals on and jump into my car on that hot summer

The little trips around town, the endless errands...

day. But usually I change into riding clothes, unchain the bike, get it out, warm it up, put on my helmet and gloves and ride.

At the post office I open my box and wrestle out all the stuff that's crammed into it. Ah, here's a new *Rider*. I lean on one of the high tables and try to read my column as if I'd never seen it before. What would I think of it if I hadn't written it? Buy some stamps from the nice lady at the window. "Hi, Grace On your bike today?" I've lived in this small town for 30 years; everybody knows everybody. It's a nice feeling.

Back out from the dim, cool, echoing lobby into the hot sun. The mail goes into my saddlebag. Helmet and gloves back on.

(Yes, gloves, even in the summer. One bad road racing crash was enough to show me what the pavement can do to your hands even *with* gloves.) Over to the town square. Chat with the pharmacist and the clerk in the drugstore. "On the bike today, Grace?"

When I first started riding, I was so proud of being a motorcyclist that I never locked my helmet on the bike; I always carried it into stores and restaurants no matter how many packages I might have to carry or how inconvenient it might be. Only very gradually did I begin to leave it behind so that now people generally have to ask.

Packages into the saddlebags. Helmet on, etc. Down to the shopping plaza next. Around the peaceful little village green with the kamikaze traffic, stop at the light. An older man pulls alongside in his car, gives my bike a long look, nods his head pleasantly.

"Nice bike. Is it new?"

"No, it's a '75."

"Boy, it sure looks brand new."

I smile proudly. He tells me about the old Indian he used to have. (It's a *very* long light.) Then we turn in our different directions with a wave and a smile. So many pleasant conversations like that.

Down the hill to the plaza. Helmet off, etc. To the bank. "Hi, Grace," the teller says. "On your bike today?"

"Oh yes. What's new and exciting in your life?" I ask as I always do, always hoping to hear something wonderful. "Nothing," she says.

You could get a motorcycle, I feel like saying, but don't. "Well, hang in there," I say instead.

Walking down to the dimestore I glance over at where my bike is parked, gleaming white and silver in the sun. A man is standing there, looking at it with a little boy. The man gestures as if he's explaining something. I can't stand not being there, being acknowledged as the owner of that marvelous machine, so I stroll casually over as if that's what I'd intended to do anyhow.

"Nice bike!" says the little boy eagerly. "Is it yours?"

"Yes, it is," I say smiling at him, and another pleasant conversation takes place — maybe my mini-lecture on safe riding.

Finally I get to the dimestore. "Hi, Grace. You on your bike today?"

More packages. Another saddlebags-helmet-gloves routine. On and off the bike. On and off. Two blocks away, stop again

Every errand is a little challenge. The traffic. The parking space. Checking the surface. Moving the bike out again. Back into traffic. I feel like an athlete practicing the same familiar and beloved moves over and over. I try to do them with flair and finesse Sometimes I make an awkward move and hope no one was watching — kick my saddlebag when I swing a leg over, or ride off and steer instead of lean, or have a foot slip in a gravel parking space when I'm trying to push the bike, or leave one saddlebag open and flapping.

But although we all have that occasional sense of "Gee, I'm not riding very well today," most of the time I feel smooth and comfortable. I feel the satisfaction that comes with making a well-executed physical move. Sitting on the bike for hours on the open road has a mystique all its own. But learning to be at home on the bike comes from all that climbing on and off, all those starts and stops, all those parking places.

The little trips around town, the endless errands over the years are like a non-stop education that helps keep my riding skills sharp. "The good Lord willin'," as Arthur Godfrey used to say, I hope to go to school forever.

Rider July 1980

Visiting the Past

I hadn't seen Uncle Earl in many years, nor Aunt Edith for even longer. Earl was my mother's older brother, and six years ago when I visited them in Elizabethtown, New York, where they lived on 160 acres in the Adirondacks, it was like a trip into the past: reminiscences about my parents, now dead; the house full of old books and photos, home-canned food and love; the yard full of woods and mountains, fish ponds, wood piles, and hard work. And on the dresser in the room where I slept was Earl's big-game hunting license. He was 85 years old.

In the two days I spent there, I soon learned that Earl was a biker from way back. Way, way back. The stories started from the moment I rode into the yard and he came out to help me unload. I was uncertain about how much help to let him give me. He was six feet tall, a little unsteady on his feet, and so thin that, skinny as I am, I felt husky by comparison. I took the big pack off the back of my bike and gave him a small bag that I had my leathers wrapped in.

"You think I can carry this OK?" he asked wryly. I chuckled a little to myself. I had a lot to learn about Earl.

I learned that he could still walk through the woods that he'd walked for so many years. And even though I frequently reached out a hand to steady him, I always stopped short of touching his arm, for I saw that he didn't need it. I learned that he put up a huge wood pile every year and ran his own snow blower and helped Edith with the hard parts of the gardening. And I learned that he'd owned two motorcycles: 1914 and 1915 Excelsiors.

I learned that women passengers used to ride sidesaddle when they dared to ride at all. And I can picture the great arc through the air made by my Aunt Edith in her immaculate khaki riding dress and her descent into a miraculously placed pile of leaves after Earl had gassed "the machine," as he called it, through a mud puddle only to learn too late of the rut lurking beneath the murky water.

...The difference between them..."One's black and one's white...."

I learned about the flat tire he'd had just outside Niagara Falls. He had no spare tube with him, and his attempts at patching didn't work. Every half mile the patch would work loose, so he finally gave up and started waving down passing bikers. A number of riders stopped, but none had a spare tube. "So I finally gave this one guy five dollars and asked him to ride to the Falls and buy a tube for me." Off went the good Samaritan, so, of course, the very next biker to stop had the tube that Earl needed. He was wearing it around his neck under his coat, a handy place in those days. "Well, thanks," Earl said, "but I've got a guy comin' back pretty soon — already went to get me a tube." So the innertube-bedecked Flying Merkle rider was on his way, and pretty soon indeed the other rider returned with Earl's new tube *and* all the change from the five dollars. "Trust" was the name of the game back then.

The stories kept coming, but finally I had to be on my way. As I rode off, I pictured many bike trips back there into the mountains, into those hugs, those big farm breakfasts, those berry-picking walks, and the tales of long ago motorcycling. But it wasn't to be. Aunt Edith died suddenly about a year later and Uncle Earl moved into a retirement home in Buffalo to be near his daughter, my cousin Mildred. I visited them, of course, but it wasn't the same.

Then this past summer I had an idea. I enlisted the help of my friend Dan — tall, strong, enormously capable and kind — the man who'd taught me to ride and all I know about bikes. We'd make the 200-mile trip to Buffalo, and he would take Earl for a ride. "Do you think your dad would be willing to go for a little ride?" I wrote Mildred. "Yes," she wrote back. "He says he thinks he would like that." Small as I am, I've never been keen on carrying passengers, and a 90-year-old man well, Dan would be the one. My idea, his skill — we'd make Earl the hero of all his cronies at the retirement home: a motorcycle ride after — what — sixty years?

Mildred had brought him to her house for the afternoon, and as Dan and I arrived on our BMWs, I heard Mildred exclaiming about how good-looking the bikes were and wondering what the difference between them was. "One's black and one's white," I heard Earl's laconic answer, and had to smile again. He may have been pretty sick this winter, but the old sense of humor was still there.

But he was not the same Earl this time. He appeared in the doorway, frail as a dry, silvery dandelion top waiting for a puff of wind to blow it away. I think I knew when I first saw him that the ride would never happen. He told the same bike stories again, but now they were interspersed with comments about how hard it was to walk his daily mile, and how sometimes he got dizzy when he stood up. And when the afternoon wore on towards evening with no mention of the ride, I finally had to ask. The answer was a very quiet, "No, I don't think I'd better. "

The next day as Dan and I rode on towards another destination, I said, "I hope you weren't too disappointed." I'd had to examine my own disappointment. Just think of all Earl would have had to talk about after such a ride! But the phrase "make Earl a hero" had begun to bother me. Was it Earl's needs or my own I was considering? I had imagined him saying afterwards, "Yes, my wonderful niece arranged the whole thing .... " He had his memories; maybe those were all he needed.

"No, I'm not disappointed," Dan called over to me as we headed west towards Chicago. "Any guy who'd ride a 1914 Excelsior to his own wedding and figure to get there was a hero a long time ago."

I should have thought of that.

Rider October 1980

Secret Love

Emily Dickinson (1830-1886), the elusive and reclusive Belle of Amherst, one of America's foremost poets, is frequently quoted in those endless attempts of scholars to define poetry: "If I feel physically as if the top of my head were taken off, I know that is poetry." Long-suppressed evidence now reveals that she may actually have been a road-race groupie and have written that line standing in the pits next to her boyfriend while he revved up his TZ250 Yamaha after tinkering with its recalcitrant carburetor: "Low at my problem bending! Another problem comes ... " she wrote, obviously referring to her lover's frustrations as he worked.

Emily's much-studied secret love notwithstanding, I have my own secret love to confess in spite of all my public protestations to the contrary. Even in spite of the wonderfully quiet motorcycle I ride and praise to the skies, even in spite of the obscenities I direct at the uncouth ruffians who shatter the silence of a peaceful neighborhood with their unmuffled manifestations of macho, I secretly love nearly all the sounds a motorcycle is capable of making.

My friends with their Grand Prix bikes at the Nelson Ledges road race course, the pipes like sticks of continuously exploding dynamite, lifted the top of my head off too. When we pitted together, all the excitement I felt about racing my own RD250 in the relatively sedate Production Class would be momentarily washed away in the shrieking, nearly tangible inundation of sound that blotted out absolutely everything in the brain except itself. Even turning away appalled, with my hands over my ears, I still felt a thrill to think that soon a rider would actually straddle that screaming beast and make it do his bidding with a twist of the wrist.

"Any guy who'd ride a 1914 Excelsior to his own wedding and figure to get there was a hero a long time ago."

"The World feels dusty ... Honors taste dry ... " Emily must have hung out at the motocross track too. I'd never heard such a peculiar sound as that emanating from the dusty pits that first-ever Sunday at the races. The first bike that was started up next to me sounded like a bunch of stones being shaken violently in a huge tin can.

Having buzzed the 30 miles to the track on what was then my street bike, a Suzuki GT250, and thinking (rather proudly) that I was making a fair amount of noise myself (do we all feel that way on our first bikes?), I was dumbfounded at the sounds of MX racing. Surely no one would come away from there with a vestige of hearing left. Little did I know I'd soon own one of those little stones-in-a-tin-can-powered banshees myself, and somehow I can still hear as well as ever. Huh?

Late on a quiet, hot summer night in the rural area where I live, I sit on my screened-in porch or lie in bed just before sleep and picture the chase scene over on the state route half a mile away. Two big Hondas (whose stock pipes lasted no longer than the trip home from the dealer's), their deep, hollow, lion-like, moaning roar rolling through the darkness, poke holes in the distant night, following that thin golden alley of light towards the black and mysterious horizon always just beyond. Never, never would I ride at night at those speeds, but vicariously I experience the blurred black rush of pavement beneath me and wrap the suddenly shuddering chill of the night air around me like some kind of armor, making myself invincible, invisible except for a shining yellow eye that always thinks it will see the peril that lurks on the midnight highway.

My neighbor's immaculate 1972 Suzuki triple, clatters and rattles its way through its warmup as he prepares for an evening ride after work. The chain saw buzz of the dirt bike up the road echoing through the woods and fields as it darts from hill to mud hole to tractor rut to home and out again. The soft, puttering whir of Dan's downshifting as he turns into my driveway on his BMW. The thunderous rumble of an outlaw caravan riding outrageously down my quiet country road, sedately observing the speed limit, endlessly and ominously filling the whole half-mile stretch in front of my house, as amazing an apparition as I (and the cows along the pasture fences) have ever seen or heard.

The breastbone-vibrating, throat-tightening, bottomless bass throb of the only Ducati in the 24-Hours of Nelson. The hard, clean-cut pulse of an old Triumph going by on an early spring afternoon. My friend down the road, a successful road race privateer tuning for the next race, making a fairly illegal 100-mile-an-hour pass down the long straight stretch between his house and mine, his TZ750 sounding like a prolonged blast on the

Doomsday trumpets while I wait for the sonic boom. "What idiocy!" I think righteously. ("Wow!" I think simultaneously.)

I know — he has no right to ride like that on the street. Not this street anyhow. But the *sound* of that engine! Close on the fading echoes of the TZ comes the murmuring purr of a portly Gold Wing and soon after that the spritely hum of a skinny little mo-ped. The solitary chugging of a Harley, the shrill buzzing whine of a small two-stroke in its cloud of blue smoke. The sounds of *those* engines please me too.

I have a foot in two camps. Must be my Libra rising, or so an astrologer told me once. I'm as indignant as everyone else at the assault on my eardrums of unmuffled exhausts on any vehicle, including lawnmowers. There oughtta be a law! My own bike is as quiet as they come, and I wouldn't have it any other way. And yet ... and yet. "The farthest Thunder that I heard/ was nearer than the Sky ... " You know it, Emily! The original Motorcycle Mama! It was right down the road. Over the river and through the woods. Around the track and around the corner. From the white whisper of my own BMW to the midnight moan of the distant Hondas, I love 'em all.

Rider November 1980

Better Off at Home

Have you ever taken a trip that you just plain should never have taken? — not that any real disasters occurred, but everything just felt wrong. My recent trip into the Catskill Mountains of New York was one such trip. Better I should have stayed home and mowed the lawn.

An old friend suddenly got in touch with me this past winter after 12 years. We'd been part of an intense group of struggling poets back in the mid-'60s, then had gone our separate ways. Now here he was again after all this time, inviting me to visit him and his girlfriend at his home in the Catskills. Sounded like a mountain paradise. I said I might like to ride up, come good weather.

But with one thing and another, the summer began to slip away. An earlier bike trip to Buffalo and Chicago with a friend had seemed like trip enough for a while, and one more was in the offing to visit my younger son who manages a marina on Chesapeake Bay. No, I finally decided to let the jaunt into the mountains go for this year. The beginning of school was not far away; work was piling up. I really didn't have the time, and no real plans had been made anyhow.

And then a phone call from my friend: "Hey, when are you coming? We're waiting to see you." Seems he'd interpreted my maybes and ifs as This Summer For Sure. Darn. I really didn't feel like going. The 500 miles wasn't so much the issue: The distance wasn't great and the scenery would be beautiful. The timing just felt off — not in my engine but in my head.

Come on Grace, I said to myself. You're not all that busy. Get packed up. Go Enjoy. Relax. Reluctantly I started to get my gear together. That's when it all started. I decided to set up my tent just to check it out. I hadn't used it in about two years, for my last couple of trips had been with a friend. As I tried to unroll it, it stuck to itself as if it were covered with glue. What *was* this stuff all over it? Had it been sprayed with something that had reacted badly with its ripstop nylon surface? Was it some kind of natural aging process? Do tents get senile? Well, I didn't have much choice; it'd have to do for now. Into my pack it went, along with all the other old familiar stuff that I'd learned makes for a good trip.

Might as well do this up right, I thought as I was getting ready to leave the next morning, straining to feel the excitement I'd felt about other trips. Full leathers and my full face helmet. Well, the leathers lasted about 15 minutes before I was drenched with sweat just walking from the garage to the house and back as I loaded the bike in near 90-degree heat. My bad mood won out over self-protection. Off they came and into my pack, and on went my old corduroy riding jacket and pants.

The full face helmet lasted a little longer — about 10 miles down the road. I'd used it for racing in the past and never thought of it as uncomfortable. But somehow it now clamped my head in a vice-like grip; the newly added visor and shield (which I thought I'd road-tested adequately) made wind noise that sounded like getting hit on the head with an erratic hammer. Five hundred miles like that and I'd be ready for a straitjacket! I turned around and went back home with a huge amount of annoyance and a severe headache, put on my old helmet and goggles, and was finally off. Again.

Route 90 through Pennsylvania struck me as absolutely horrible. Weeds grew up along the sides and median strip as if the road had been abandoned long ago. Chuckholes and patches added to the eerie, deserted effect This unkempt concrete slab was taking me off to nowhere. "Kachunk, kachunk" went the seams of this seedy highway under my wheels in a monotonous and irritating rhythm.

Route 17 through southern New York, a road I'd ridden once before and remembered as quite beautiful, somehow gave me the creeps. It too seemed empty and desolate to match my state of mind. The blue sky, the ever-higher hills did nothing to improve my mood; I scarcely glanced at them as I rode grumpily along.

Since I'd gotten such a late start, I didn't plan to do the whole trip in one day. I camped that might, wrestling my stuck-together tent out of its love affair with itself, wrestling with my nerves as I do every first night out on the road (What's that noise in the woods?), wrestling with an extremely rare case of violent indigestion or something — was it the cucumbers in the salad at that restaurant down the road, or was it just all-round bad vibes?

The next day my friend's driveway turned out to be a perpendicular ascent of dirt and loose shale that absolutely freaked me out. How would I ever get up? How would I ever get down again if it rained? His mountain paradise was completely dominated by two wildly shedding dogs and needed cleaning very badly, and the old friendship just didn't seem to be there anymore. Tensions built up; we quarreled about virtually everything; it did rain. Why on earth had I ever come? I left a day ahead of schedule, plunged without incident down the nightmarish driveway, and rode home (home!) in one 10-hour stretch.

Route 17 now seemed absolutely gorgeous, and it magically avoided the thunderstorms that were charging blackly towards me all day from the southwest. Even Route 90 was now a marvelous high-speed olden days highway; all traffic was clipping along freely at about 70 mph, including me. Not a patrol car to be seen in 500 miles! I scarcely moved a muscle the whole way, perched on my motorcycle feeling perfectly balanced on the bike and in the world. *Now* things felt right. I could have ridden a thousand miles that day, I think, just in relief at getting away and heading home

In this business, all trips are somehow supposed to be mystical excursions off into the sunset so that we can write about them in rhapsodic prose for our readers. But this trip — I never should have gone. The little voice was telling me that all along. The pressure of work, the false starts, the indigestion — the time was wasted, the friendship severely damaged, and I learned that my older son had totaled his car the day I left!

Bio-rhythms? The conjunction of the planets? The phase of the moon? Who knows? Next time I'll check out the tarot cards, the Ouija board, and the lines in my hand first, then I'll ask myself, "Grace, do you *really* want to go on this trip?" And if that little voice says no, I'll listen.

Rider December 1980

New Perceptions

What we are born knowing via genetic code or what we can experience through mystical awareness is still up for study. And while the intellect is indeed a wondrous apparatus, or process, or dimension, whatever the word might be, nearly all our acquisition of knowledge is through our five senses. For the long-time motorcyclist, the sheer sensuous pleasure of riding is always high on the list of reasons for indulging. But for the beginning biker, the impact on the senses, the strange new perceptions, can be almost overwhelming.

The on-the-earth heaviness of my first motorcycle seemed astonishing to me after having watched experienced riders handle their bikes with a flick of the wrist, a mere bulge of the bicep, a thrust of the thigh. My 250 Suzuki seemed to weigh a thousand pounds and, strong as I always thought I was, pushing it around produced instant trembling and a wild prickling of sweat. The ominous words, "What if I drop it?" pulsed in my head as if in an echo chamber, and the thought of the gleaming plum-colored tank with a horrible and incriminating dent in it hovered over all my tense maneuverings.

Then there was the first time I ever put gas in my own bike — the awkward struggle with the heavy, unruly hose and nozzle — being on the wrong side of the pumps to have my stronger right hand do most of the work as I sat on my bike. Wrist aching, the trigger seeming uncontrollable under my inexperienced fingers, I managed to fill the tank. I had never so much as put gas in my own car, let alone performed the delicate operation of topping off a bike tank with a hose that seemed about as cooperative as a captive anaconda.

Washing a motorcycle, too, was a mysterious business at first — all those nooks and crannies compared to the broad, smooth, curving surfaces of a car. You actually hosed down the *seat?* The engine? Poured soap and water over the *engine?* Got it *wet?* The acrid smell of engine degreaser — and learning that it eats blacktop driveways for dessert. And then the drying, the polishing, my skinny fingers exploring all those silvery crevices, learning as if by Braille those around-in-backs and the in-unders And the sleepy hours in the sun when it was polish-the-spokes time.

I remember feeling like a child the first time I put a helmet on — the strange white stiffness of it — and couldn't figure out how those D-ring fasteners worked out of sight up there under my chin. Seemed to be at least six rings and three straps for a while. Had to stand there, four years old again, while a grown-up fastened my hat on for me.

I had no windshield on my bike in my first weeks of riding, and that first solo out of the parking lot and up the hill in the nearby state park introduced me to the devastating force of the wind in my face and against my body as I roared (lurched?) away from my instructor. Swooping up the road, leaning forward against the invisible frenzy of this new adversary, stunned by my daring, I risked a glance at the speedometer so I could brag about how fast I'd gone my first time alone on the bike. What? Twenty-five miles an hour? Holy cow! At 50 I'd be swept away as surely as by a hurricane!

Discovering on still summer nights the sudden cold dark pockets of air in the little valleys and climbing out of them, goose bumps subsiding, had me alternately cold and warm like a thermostat going on and off. Some of those dark pools were so cold they'd make me gasp and tense up inside my leather jacket, the chill moonlight like an electric probe running its shocking fingers down the back of my neck, down my spine, down to my toes curled tightly inside my boots as I tried not to shiver. Surely bikers didn't shiver. Shivering wasn't cool!

I rode through the scent of summer hayfields or cigar smoke from the car ahead, past pig farms and by charcoal-broiling steaks, among pines and beside sewage treatment plants, on the outskirts of steel mills and into the pungent yards of cider mills, my mind whirling to take it all in, record it, remember it.

Oncoming trucks would slide by as smoothly as ocean liners or wallop me with a sledge hammer of turbulence, and rain grooves would startle me into a rigor mortis of controlled tension or slip under my wheels as if merely painted on the road. Steel grate bridges gaped suddenly under me, sending me into a hypnotic state of concentration born of terror as I tried not to look through the meshwork into the river below, the bike wobbling its way across,

But I also remember that fall day when I finally walked from a store and over to my bike and swung a leg over it with no awareness at all. I just sat there in the sun for a blank peaceful moment before I realized that for the first time, sitting on my bike had a feeling of relief about it, like coming home after being away for a long time, My helmet was fastened, the spokes were polished, the wind was my friend, the smell of hamburgers from a nearby McDonald's merely reminded me that I was hungry, and I pushed the bike back out of the parking space with no concern except for the oncoming traffic.

As a beginner I felt an intensity of physical sensation so great as to seem almost an overdose; now I still have the same perceptions when I ride but in a more manageable and less exhausting form. As a Zen master once put it, "At first the mountains and trees are just mountains and trees. As one proceeds toward enlightenment, they become so much more than mountains and trees. And then they are just mountains and trees again." But never in quite the same way, I might add, once the sensuous world of motorcycling opened up to let me in.

Rider January 1981

On Motorcycles Through Amish Country

That late bright afternoon
we rode the boundary line
between winter and spring
along the edge of the equinox,
the sun warm on our backs,

the air cold on our faces.

The other boundary line we rode
was between centuries,
past houses dug by hand
deep into the ground,

not tied to this world
by any wires,
curtained with a curious silence.

We slid through the ancient air
quietly, invisible.
Only the children,
waving and smiling,
could see us
while their fathers carried
heavy pails in and out
of the splendid barns
and their mothers washed and hung
the simple clothes.

In the fields, the huge horses
pulled a silver thread
through the dark seams
of the opening earth.

We drifted along the twisting roads,
sun flickering off the strange chrome
of our slow and intricate machines.

Later, back on the highway,
we leaped into 80 miles an hour
as if to break through into
our own world again,
but we throttled off in apology
for disturbing the setting sun

as if we were still back
on those slow roads

where the good people
sleep with the darkness,
rise with the light
to don their somber black,
their muted colors.

When we ride through again
years from now,
nothing will have changed.

And we will have
that strange sense

of having returned home
to a place
we do not belong.

from *Before I Go Out on the Road*
Cleveland State University Poetry Center 1979

Paranoia

    My first observations of the limitless horizons of motorcycling were from the back seat of a BMW R75/5, a big black mount that I viewed with the misty eyes of a medieval maiden gazing at the noble steed of her favorite knight in armor. For about a month I rode passenger, watching all the moves my friend Dan made, listening to his comments on safe riding, his explanations of why he did this or didn't do that. I soaked up all the bike stories and remembrances he and his friend Stub swapped as we sat over coffee in some restaurant we'd ridden to together. I basked in the mystique of this new and exciting world, soon to be my own as I would be buying my first bike about a month later.
    But I gradually became aware of a peculiar tension that hovered over our excursions and that soon enough would become part of my own life. As we'd pull into the parking lot and dismount on a peaceful, sunny Sunday afternoon to hike some trails in a beautiful park, Dan would look up with narrowed eyes and say to Stub, "Check out that van." "I see him," Stub would

answer. I'd see the van too, of course, as it circled the parking lot, driver giving us a nonchalant glance, but I didn't see anything ominous about it — just another couple of guys cruising the park, stereo blaring, looking for girls, I supposed. "What about the van?" I'd ask, wondering what they saw that I didn't.

Or we'd stop at a restaurant, and they would choose a parking space with what seemed an inordinate amount of planning and discussion. What difference did it make where we parked? "Think we can see 'em from here?" "Yeah, this'll be OK."

Soon enough I saw the light. What about the van? A couple of guys in a van could easily enough shove an unlocked, unguarded bike into it and drive away. The parking place at the restaurant? Same thing. You didn't leave a good looking bike parked out of sight if you could help it; it just might not be there when you came out. Full stomach, empty parking place equals one bad case of indigestion.

About two weeks after I got my first bike, my neighbor, who just happened to be up at 2 a.m., saw someone go into my garage. "Outta gas. Just wondered if you had any I could borrow," was the stranger's explanation when my neighbor confronted him. "Borrow" some gas? Or "borrow" my new bike? Just coincidence that my new bike and the stranger happened to be in my garage at the same time? An elaborate alarm system for my garage was my next major purchase.

I've passed up restaurants that have no windows, campsites that force me to leave my bike elsewhere and hike in, visits to friends who live on tenth floors of apartments. For those I take my car.

I was never paranoid about anything in my life before, but first impressions are hard to shake. All those stories of stolen bikes I heard from all sides when I was a beginner really hit me hard. I guess much of my attitude depends on where I am — in what part of the country — my mood — some kind of instinctive feeling that here my bike and all my gear are safe, but here I wouldn't let them out of my sight.

At one motel I laboriously push the bike right up to the window and run my long chain right into the room and around a table leg. At least I'll hear the noise if somebody starts hacking away at it at 3 a.m. Once I'm ready for bed and have turned the lights out, I'll open the motel curtains so I can see the bike from my bed. But at another I'll leave the bike and walk up the road to dinner without a second thought.

In one restaurant I'll get up three times to go take a look because I couldn't park the bike in sight of a window. At another I'll eat a leisurely meal and linger over coffee with scarcely a thought of bike snatchers. Who knows why. So far, so good (knock on wood).

Paranoia is not my middle name, but hey, isn't that the second time that blue van just cruised by? And hasn't that car been behind us ever since we left the restaurant? Let's not pull in my driveway; I don't want that guy to know where my motorcycle lives!

Rider February 1981

Daydreaming

What must it be like, I've often wondered, to live where people ride motorcycles all year and can really say that bikes are their major form of transportation? And has the weather changed, or have I? How come the first winter I ever rode, I managed to put 4,000 miles on my bike between the end of October and the first of April? Did it really not snow much that winter or the one after that? Did I somehow *will* it not to snow then so I could ride straight through my first winter as a biker? So that buying my first bike at the end of October turned out not to be a dumb thing to do? So that my momentum as an eager beginner wouldn't get lost in the snowdrifts of northeastern Ohio?

No, it didn't snow much those first two winters, but it sure has since then, and I still have never quite "Put the bike away for the winter." Oh, there are many weeks when, from half a mile away, I hear the roaring, scraping sounds of the sparking plow blade over pavement still bare in places as road crews fight to hold back the white waves that surge across empty roads by windswept fields. But in the dim corner of my garage my beloved machine gleams quietly, and I put down my snow shovel and pretend I am going to ride.

I sit daydreaming on the motionless bike, my breath white out in front of me. There is no panorama of scenery here, no mountains or lakes or curving roads wound tightly on a spindle to unwind behind me just like in the movies. There is no giant fan to blow my hair back or ripple my shirt. There are only the bare walls of this nowhere garage huddled under the onslaught of yet another storm.

But I sit astride my bike, carefully watching the road that seems to lie ahead. I move forward into a spring I've never known, knowing exactly how it will be: those flowers in a field far to the east and twilights that do not have four walls around them.

Soon I will not be sitting in a daydream which is unthinkable on the real road, for death smells just like plowed fields and looks just like the green haze on the trees. The cold creeping into my unmoving toes and fingers gradually rouses me, but I feel somehow happy as I dismount, lock up, trudge through the snow back to the house, shoveling snow forgotten. I have just ridden to somewhere, more or less. For now, that's all there is, I guess.

But suddenly on a cold, bright Sunday afternoon in January comes a phone call. "Hi! Ya wanna ride?" I am delighted, but feel obliged to inform my friend that it's 25 degrees outside. "Yeah, I know." And 15 minutes later I hear the ka-chug ka-chug of a big old Harley in my drive. Walking stiffly out, heavily swaddled in all my cold-weather riding gear, I greet him, warm up my own bike, and we take off. Half an hour out we find that inevitable cup-of-coffee-piece-of-pie. We linger over bike talk: he reminisces about the days when he was a carnival biker riding the motordromes, those creaking old wooden silo-like structures, climbing nearly to the top of the almost perpendicular walls where the customers would be peering over the edge, then diving to the bottom, and climbing again. I listen like a child, enthralled.

Out of the restaurant into the shock of the cold air, I start to shiver instantly, but the chill passes, and the half hour back home seems short. Motorists, enclosed in their isolated worlds, turn uncomprehending eyes towards us thinking how we must suffer! They will never know from their heated and defrosted seats how our bodies in their leather skins move easily through the frozen air. They will never understand the power that rumbles, hot as volcanoes, ready to be released with one flick of a gloved hand, or the one glance connecting us across the thin, sharp edges of the air. They cannot believe that we would ride to nowhere for the sheer cold crazy joy of it. They stare. We smile with stiff faces, spinning down the miles ahead of the snow, thinking of the cup of coffee always at the end of the road, and of all the brilliant, cold, and splendid roads we know.

And then finally, something happens — not the next day, maybe, or the next week, but soon enough. A gray, 40-degree day in long-ago October may have seemed too frigid for riding after the sensuous summer months, but a 40-degree day in February when an unseasonably hard rain has washed the salt from the roads, and the snowbanks lining the highways seem blurred and smaller, and a narrow path has melted itself through the ice covering my driveway — why, that's almost spring!

High warm winds will sweep the land for a day, and like crocuses in snow, motorcycles will bloom like sudden flowers on the drab winter roads, or like red and blue and orange butterflies emerging from the gray cocoons of garages. Carefully down the tiny bare pathway, both feet down like outriggers over the ice, just enough space for my tires to fit, and out onto the road — I am riding! Memory stirs in wrists and thighs; curves call like Lorelei; leather soaks up hungrily what feels like the first-ever sun in the world.

Other bikers pass: we wave; we are like lovers with the strange warm air. We ride too fast, too far, and are caught miles from home by the cold clamping down of twilight. Is that just water or is it ice on the darkening road? What's the temperature? Scary. Get home! But be careful. We return, shivering and subdued.

Tomorrow the air turns to snow again. We put ourselves away. But it's as if this one day awakened us from some kind of sleep. We only doze now, waiting for it to all happen again.

Rider March 1981

All Alone

"What do you do when you're all alone on a camping trip?" people ask me from time to time. "I started on a trip alone once," a reader writes, "and turned around and went back, I was so lonely." "The riding part's OK, but being alone in a campsite really bums me out," another reader says. Or, "Eating meals by myself — I feel so conspicuous — kind of lost."

Well, let me think back on my trips alone and recall not only some of the things I do when I'm alone on the road, but, maybe more important, the mood or attitude in which I do them. I think a lot of people are missing out on a lot of good trips for fear that going alone would be just plain awful. On the contrary, it can be just plain wonderful.

First, when the friend with whom you've been planning the trip says all of a sudden that he or she can't go, try not to get angry. Try not to be sad. Don't panic or cancel the trip. Try feeling relieved. Haven't you always secretly longed to have everything your own way? Now's your chance. You can ride only as far as you want on any given day, eat when you want, turn where you want, stay wherever you want as long as you want. You're the boss.

Or maybe you've planned the trip alone from the beginning, but as the time approaches, you're getting a little uneasy. You're having a "what if" attack. But *every* day is fraught with potential danger; all those what if's are just as likely to happen on your way to work. Acknowledge them but set them aside. I always hate it when someone comes up to me on the starting line of a race, pats me on the back, and mutters, "Now don't be nervous." What a ridiculous thing to say. I'd much rather have that person say, realistically, "I'll bet you're pretty nervous, huh? That's OK; so's everybody else. Go get 'em!" So be nervous, worry about the what if's. But go!

Now, how about a non-human companion for this trip. I'm going to suggest something, and you're going to say, "Oh yeah, sure, that's fine for you; you're a writer." But it's fine for you too. Try it once. Take along a brand-new, empty notebook (a fairly large one) and a couple of pens. And every day when you're off the road into a campsite or a field or a motel, and your chores are done, and you start wondering with some anxiety what to do with yourself for the rest of the evening, sit down and begin to write about the events of the day. And even more important than the events, write about your thoughts and feelings.

Whether or not you're a "good" writer is totally irrelevant; it's the act of writing that's important. And "important" is a key word here, because the very act of keeping a journal on your trip will somehow make everything you do seem *very* important. Your thoughts, the trip itself will become, in a way, immortal once given permanence on a piece of paper, especially if you write with a pen and not a pencil.

You will, in effect, be writing your own little book. Nobody's going to grade it; you don't have to worry about spelling or punctuation or grammar. And to your surprise, you may find that the physical act of writing is a soothing, comforting thing to do. The time goes very fast; you become absorbed; it is as if you're talking to someone — the imaginary someone who might read this someday and relive and wonder at and enjoy this experience of yours.

And each day as you ride, see sights, talk to people, you'll find yourself making mental notes so you can remember to write about these things later. Or you may stop at a rest area just to record the wonderful thoughts you had a few miles ago. The whole trip seems to take on a different feeling, a different dimension, almost as if you're making the trip *in order* to write about it; you seem to have acquired a purpose for the trip, even a reason for being alone; you're off on a great adventure. The world (or at least your grandchildren) may someday read this little book, and you will have created something that someone in the future may get pleasure from. You will probably read it again and be surprised at how memories leap out at you in a wonderful kind of way.

Take the journal into restaurants with you; jot down bits and pieces of the day's ride so far; your uncertainty about which route to take a few miles back down the road or your first glimpse of a moose disappearing into the misty woods. You will feel not conspicuous but interesting — people will wonder who you might be and what you might be writing about. There will be an aura of mystery about you. You can gaze off into space, nibble on the pen between sips of coffee, then smile and write down a few more words. Nod your head as you re-read what you've just written. Flip back a few pages to yesterday's entry. What were you thinking about then? How does it compare to your mood today? Nod your head again as you complete this important piece of research. Record for posterity the fact that you have just finished your Big Mac and will now start on the large order of fries. Think how future generations may puzzle over these cryptic entries; scholars may ponder their meaning; books may be written about your book: *Interpretations of the Ancient Biker's Trip Book and Its Implications for Modern Society* (Or: "Who Was Big Mac?").

I'm getting a little carried away here. But truly, you will be surprised at what a friend such a notebook can become.

Sometimes it can even serve a practical purpose such as allowing you to look up the exact route you took in order to recommend it to a friend or to retrace it yourself someday. Or it may provide an important date or an address. And you will be surprised, too, at how much of that free time you were so worried about can be taken up by writing a play-by-play account of a day's travels. It's a relaxing thing to do after dark by the light of a candle lantern at a picnic table near your tent, or in a motel when there's nothing any good on the TV that doesn't work very well anyhow. A pen can feel good between your fingers when it's creating something almost like a work of art that'll be around long after you're gone.

That empty notebook turns into a kind of mirror as it fills with your thoughts, your images. As long as you have a blank piece of paper that can reflect who you are and where you've been, you'll never be alone.

Rider April 1981

Anticipation

"Made any long trips?" — the inevitable question directed to owners of certain kinds of motorcycles equipped in certain ways. Having to say "Not yet" feels uncomfortable. We have not done that which we ought to have done. Being able to answer "Sure have!" and proceeding to tell the questioners all they ever wanted to know but were afraid to ask about motorcycle touring is almost a reward in itself.

In theory, I could go anywhere in the U.S. I wanted to, for I have three months off from teaching every summer — one of the fantastic fringe benefits of the teaching profession (not much money, but oh, that beautiful Free Time!). So somewhere in between the last trip and the next one, ideas and images start moving through my mind. A friend in Oklahoma sends her annual Christmas letter. We've known each other since we were about five and haven't been together since maybe 1960. "When are you coming out here?" she asks every year.

The camera moves rapidly back and up; the film is obviously being shot from a helicopter. Act 47: Scene 9,872: Lone Motorcyclist heads west through the flat farmlands of Ohio, riding toward emotional reunion with Old Childhood Friend.

Next scene shows Lone Motorcyclist and Old Childhood Friend embracing on OCF's threshhold while children of OCF stand shyly around the LM in awe of Mommie's Brave Friend who has come all this way to see them. (Actually, OCF's children are all grown up and married and gone from home now, but it makes a better scene this way.)

Or there's that *Road Not Taken* (thank you, Robert Frost) that curled along beside that silvery river in Quebec. I'm still wondering what influenced my decision on that day. What adventure might have happened along that road? Maybe I could go back and start another trip in the middle of that old one. I don't know, though. "You can't repeat the past," Nick says in *The Great Gatsby*. (Thank you, F Scott Fitzgerald.)

Route 1 along the ocean in California — I've read so often about bikers racing along its curving length that riding it would seem like a *deja* vu experience. And finally the redwoods and sequoias — the towering pine by my house would seem small when I came back.

Should I make a loop around the outskirts of the whole U.S. with little side trips into the interior? Should I ride straight through the middle of the U.S. with little side trips to the exterior? Or something I think would be a great trip: sort of a saturation tour of my own state, exploring every nook and cranny it has to offer. Ohio has a tremendous variety of terrain, from the big hills (low old mountains, really) of southern Ohio to the New England-like northeast corner, and the "prairies," you could say, heading flatly on over into Indiana. As a participant in the Poets in the Schools program, I crisscrossed the state in my car for several years thinking, "Gee, I wish I were on my bike!" Now, free of briefcase, books, and other poet paraphernalia, I could really see some of those interesting areas I hurried through on my way to one school or another.

I get out a box of maps. Some are so old they don't even have the freeways on them. Have to sort all these out one of these days. Let's see — here's a map of the whole U.S. I feel an incredible surge of excitement as I spread it out on the old round oak table in the kitchen. I could hang it up on the wall, have someone blindfold me, spin me around, and point me towards the map with a pin in my hand. Wherever I stuck it, that's where I'd go.

Adrenaline surges violently through me as I picture myself leaving. I could go to the national rally. I've never been to one —

feel a little put off by the thought of camping among so many people. Yet imagine seeing a thousand BMWs gathered in one place! Must be an amazing sight. I'll bet I'd probably enjoy myself. (Even the Lone Motorcyclist has to get together with folks once in a while!)

Florida in the summer is gawd-awful hot, but there's a certain beloved Aunt Dorothy down there I'd love to hug. Late May, early June wouldn't be so bad. And on the way I could stop in Maryland and visit my sailboat-builder son, Dan. Whew — more adrenaline! Does everybody get this excited just looking at maps? Funny — out on the road, I'm pretty calm. It's this thinking about going that puts my nervous system in such a furor.

But the maps! I don't think they should dispense those things without a prescription.

Unfolding the maps is what does it. From that neat little rectangle suddenly accordions out a vast body of land covered with those red and blue veins and arteries, all pulsing with imminent adventure, sunsets to ride off into (it's never raining in our motorcycle trip fantasies), and a new column down every road.
Actually, I suppose I could just ride and ride, get where I'm going, have a nice time, and come back home — simple as that.

And sometimes that's pretty much the way it happens. But the maps! I don't think they should dispense those things without a prescription. I get so high just looking at them that — well, when the government finds out, I'm sure maps will be declared an illegal substance. Possession will be punishable by six weeks of confinement to a K-Mart parking lot.

("Pssstt! Hey buddy, ya wanna buy a map? Got a good one here — only unfolded a few times by a little old lady on a BMW. It'll get ya anywhere ya wanna go! Cheap — only $500. Huh? Aw, hey, come on back — make an offer. $250? Sold! Buddy, you got yerself a *real* trip comin' up!")

Rider June 1981

With a Little Help

Another gray, cold Saturday morning — maybe 45 degrees was the best we could hope for, and rain forecast besides. But not bad, really, for the end of February.

Felt like a long time since I'd backed the bike out, down the slight slope of the garage floor, down the sudden sharp slant of the little apron and onto the gradual downhill of the rough blacktop drive. Tricky, going backwards down all those little hills.

And now out in the daylight, in the gray and dingy morning, the pipes looked dull and shabby. This day could sure use some sparkle. While my great white beast muttered and breathed its wintry breath out into the cold air, warming itself, I did a quick polish job on the pipes and gave a swipe to the rims. So what if it might rain before I got there. I wasn't going to leave the house with the bike less than immaculate.

My leather jacket was tight over my two sweaters as I leaned forward to check my turn signals and twisted back to see my brakelight flash before I pulled out onto the road. My pants were snug over my long johns. You'd think I was going a hundred miles instead of just across town (and a small town at that). My winter gloves were pretty worn. Wonder where I can find some new ones before next year. Oh — the moves — riding again! — first time since — when? — November? Engine gets raggedy on the choke. Switch it off. OK, Cold-Blooded One, go to it!

No, no, take it easy. A little tense, it's been so long. Be careful; let it come back slowly. Watch for chuckholes. The road looks like a World War II bombing raid took place here.

Too soon I'm at Dan's house. I was just getting into riding, starting to relax in the cold air, when the garage door opens magically as I ride up. There's Jim with his bike already inside and two of his friends. All ready for the master class in base-gasket installation to begin. Can't buy high-test leaded gas anymore, so lowering the compression is one way to go.

We plunge in. Jim does his bike, I do mine; Dan choreographs, directs, moves from bike to bike — a hand here, a word there. Jim's buddies pitch in where needed. Friendly bike talk flows steadily among the five of us in the warmth of the garage, the wood stove in the corner adding an occasional pleasant crackle to the conversation.

My pistons see the light of day for the first time since the cylinders enclosed them back at the factory. They poke their dark, crusty tops out into the world. I carefully scrape them clean with a wooden scraper, clean the concave chambers of the heads, put the valves on the wire wheel. I'm happy, doing all this with my friends, learning, laughing, getting dirty, a little tired as the hours go by.

Long afterward as I ride through the heavy heat of summer, images from that late winter workshop stay with me: the great silver star nuts on the pipes that need their own special wrench (four of us bought the wrench together; it floats among us from garage to garage). The gleaming cylinder walls that imprison so much power. The shock of rust under the wide clamps on the pipes. "Not on my bike!" I say, attacking it furiously with rag and polish before reassembly. The rocker arms, the simple push rods — trying to imagine the speed at which everything moves inside those rugged valve covers.

"Gee whiz, Dan," Jim says finally, getting ready to leave, "I sure do thank you for all the help." His friends have left; it's late, dark, cold, windy, raining a bit. I put on my rainsuit for my own chilly ride home, reluctantly leaving the friendly brightness, the wood stove warmth of the garage. I'm always amazed over and over at the way things come apart and miraculously go back together; amazed at the people who seem born with the skills I've only been laboriously and cautiously acquiring in recent years.

Yes, Dan, gee whiz, I sure do thank you too, and all the other people in bike shops, garages, driveways, at the track, and on the road who've taken the time to help me learn how to do these things that I've come to love so much. Now I know how to get my hands dirty, fight a rusty bolt, not be afraid to wonder how something works, and whether I might not just possibly be able to make it work just a little better with — as the song says — a little help from my friends.

Rider July 1981

Saved by Instinct

I felt like a zombie when I left the building, an area high school where I'd been invited to appear as visiting poet. Being "on stage," either in the auditorium for a performance or up front in the classroom, and introduced as something in between a rock star and a substitute teacher while turned loose to do my thing for a whole day, is always both exhilarating and exhausting.

Luckily, my poems — which seem to be a combination of motorcycling, running track, and being in love usually hold the students' attention, and I come away feeling as if maybe I've turned them on to all three. But this day I was *tired,*

And this day I had ridden to the school which was only twenty miles or so from my home. As I walked across the parking lot, saying goodbye to a few students on the way, the momentum of the day still carried me. But once I was out on the road, fatigue draped itself over me like a limp gray blanket, and the bike droned along under me with a kind of hypnotic sound that just settled me even further into myself, my attention inward ("… so tired … so tired …") instead of outward on the road.

Riding just right of the center line as I nearly always do, probably doing the speed limit on this two-lane state route, staring blankly ahead, I was looking forward to getting home, relaxing, eating — instead of looking ahead at what the pickup truck in front of me had in mind,

A line in a poem of mine about running that I had read that day says, "I can run only where I am, each step a new place of its own." A Zen master might call it "staying in the Now moment."

Or as a friend of mine would put it, "Why the &'%$# don't ya pay attention to what yer doin', ya %&#$ jerk!"

Well, I can always say that the pickup truck had neither brake lights nor turn signals. At least I don't remember seeing any. I can always say that I wasn't tailgating because I never do, always observing the two-second count rule, But I could say, too, that I was just so tired and preoccupied that I simply wasn't paying attention. At any rate, something woke me up to the fact that I was now hurtling at 55 mph or so toward the tailgate of this very obviously motionless-in-front-of-me truck waiting to turn left into a driveway. The reason it was waiting to turn left was a semi coming in the other direction, hauling you-know-what on its way to wherever.

Well now, Miss World's-Most-Careful Rider, it would appear that you are about to lose your self-appointed title in approximately two seconds. I remember feeling incredulous that this accident was going to happen. How could it happen to me? I pictured myself hitting the truck, my body flying through the air. There was obviously no way this event was going to turn out any differently. I couldn't go to the left; the pickup truck was going to turn that way, and besides, that semi would have complicated matters even more than they already were. I couldn't get from alongside the centerline to the shoulder on the right — it was too far away, and there was too little time and not enough space. And I couldn't stop. "Goodbye, World! This is it!"

But while my mind was acknowledging my fate with amazement and resignation, my body was very busy doing some rather amazing things all by itself that I was completely unaware of. I was racing motocross during that period, and the only thing I can think of is that somehow all those racing moves just happened on a totally unconscious level.

I guess I locked up everything I could get a hand or foot on, at which point I found myself still hurtling toward the back of the truck, but sideways ("OK, so now I'm going to hit it sideways instead of head-on," was the accompanying thought.) But the body, still busily at work, had some different ideas, What did I do next? Let off the brakes, I guess, for now I shot forward toward the shoulder and a whole row of mailboxes and newspaper tubes. ("Oh, I see. I'm not going to hit the truck, I'm going to crash into these instead," said my mind, ever-so-brilliantly sizing up the situation.) But the body somehow wrenched that bike around in a near ninety degree turn, missed the boxes, and sent bike, me, and what was left of my mind (which seemed to have bailed out long ago) rapidly down the narrow shoulder between the row of boxes and the stopped truck.

The semi passed, the pickup truck turned in, and I continued on down the shoulder and back onto the road in a state that can only be described as stunned.

If you offered me $100,000, there's no way in the world I would be able to deliberately perform those maneuvers. To make what amounted to two ninety degree turns slowing down from 55 mph — sliding my full dress BMW sideways and making what had to be nearly a right angle turn to the left from that position without any conscious awareness of it at all — well, I just don't know how to do that. Surely the moves must have come from racing and from every instinct of self-preservation I ever had!

I pass that spot fairly often, and the whole thing runs like one of those loop training films through my head. I try not to ride when I know in advance I'm going to be extremely tired. Or if I must, I just run that film a few times as a reminder. I'll think about being at home when I'm home, but for now I'd better just think about the road — each mile a new place of its own.

Rider August 1981

More Odds and Ends

Many months ago I asked for reader response to a column called *Odds 'n Ends* — little "tricks," if you will, that we all use to make life even more pleasant as we pleasure ride on a weekend, commute during the week, or take off down that long road. So here it is: *Son of Odds 'n Ends.* Who knows but what there will probably be a *Son of Odds 'n Ends Returns* somewhere up the line.

Ski shops as unexpected sources of cycling gear were suggested by one reader. I'd add my own "amen" to that, for gloves come in a far greater selection of sizes and styles than in the typical bike shop. Ski shops also carry a wide variety of goggles, particularly in the small sizes. They're also good sources for colorful (highly visible) nonleather yet chill-resistant jackets.

Late winter and early spring are good times for sales, just when many of us will be needing new gear.

Another reader, perturbed by long arms, sport handlebars, and short gloves, and remembering childhood snowsuits with mittens somehow fastened to the sleeves, adds an inchwide Velcro square to the inside of the glove cuff and the outside of the jacket sleeve so ever the twain shall meet.

A substitute for a sun visor in long hours of glare is a couple of strips of tape across the face shield. This reader used black electrical tape, and I'd guess other kinds might leave sticky stuff to deal with later. He used two strips, one just above eye level and one just above that.

Several readers suggested wrapping lengths of duct tape around most anything to keep it handy and avoid carrying the large roll. I wrap a bunch around a three-inch bolt, carrying it in the tool box beneath my seat, but anything would do, including parts of the bike itself. (Duct tape once held together a friend's windshield that cracked nearly in two just from hitting a chuck hole. Sounded like a rifle shot!)

A heavy spring-type paper clip can be attached to the upright on a handlebar-mounted windshield to hold letters, money or tolls, an address, etc. It could also be put on handlebars or mirror stalk.

A small snap such as at the end of a dog leash can be sewn anywhere inside clothing to hold spare keys.

Pantyhose under jeans or unlined leathers and turtle-neck dickeys for undershirts are popular additions with many readers.

Regular industrial safety glasses in various styles can be used for eye protection. And, I might add, there's whole new line of protective glasses required for indoor ball sports like squash and racquetball that would seem to be equally suitable.

If a man must be both dressed up and riding, those ankle-high hybrids — half boot, half shoe — provide protection yet look dressy. For women who want to ride to work yet not have the bother of carrying a change of clothes, a jumpsuit over a dress or skirt will work. So many modern fabrics scarcely wrinkle; the skirt can just be folded up out of the way under the jumpsuit. You'll probably still have to carry shoes, though, unless you're wearing dress boots that day.

Wetting down a denim jacket (and jeans as well) helped several readers travel comfortably in desert heat. I've always thought rather longingly of white leathers, impractical as they would seem, for greater visibility and heat reflection (not to mention a match with my bike).

Matching fairing lock and bag keys by taking the key for the bags and the lock for the fairing pocket to a locksmith will eliminate at least one of those extra keys. The same reader suggests having a dog tag made with name, address, and blood type to carry with your keys, or to wear, in case your wallet is lost or stolen in a crash. I've used one for years while running, especially out of town where no one would know who I was if I ever got hit by a car. (It can be ordered out of the back of any running magazine.) I just pin it to my shorts. One side carries my home address while on the other I put a piece of white adhesive tape and write in any temporary address where I might be staying. Not morbid, just careful.

Plastic bags of all sizes. Ah, yes. They're for stuff that doesn't get dry overnight, or the muddy shoes, or clothes that should have been washed two weeks ago, or the unprotected gear that wouldn't fit inside something. Or even for your shivering body inside the skimpy jacket you should have known better than to wear. Or tied over your boots in case of rain.

Some extra $$ — say $20 — taped somewhere onto the bike, under cover (rolled up in a pill bottle, maybe), out of sight and weather, but not out of mind, might be a welcome touch one day.

Always, always carry a rain suit, readers say, and not just for rain. You can be cold with full leathers, long johns, and a sweater. Sometimes only a rain suit on top of it all lets you stop shivering and enjoy the ride. In a pinch several sheets of newspaper as a jacket or pants liner will help.

A frequent correspondent says he fastens a powderpuff onto the bottom of his shift lever with rubber bands for a shine instead of a scuff.

One rider, suffering sunburned and swollen wrists between short gloves and jacket cuffs on a long cross-country ride, cut the tops off a pair of socks making a wristband to fill in the space.

You can buy rubber dishwashing gloves to pull on over leather gloves in the rain.

And a flattened tin can slipped into bag or fairing will provide an always available non-sink pad for the side stand on any suspect surface.

Thanks for sharing. Let's do this again someday.

Rider September 1981

Synchronicity

In 1949 the Swiss psychologist, C.G. Jung (1875-1961), wrote a foreword to a modern edition of an ancient Chinese book, *The I Ching,* a compilation of oracular pronouncements and statements of ethical values about 3000 years old. In this foreword he speaks of a "certain curious principle" that he calls "synchronicity": the coincidence of events in space and time being based on something more than chance.

That word, "synchronicity" has stuck with me, for I've experienced a few happenings involving the bike that struck me as somehow more than coincidental. They were welcome, mysterious, and "right." Trivial though each may have been, they all seemed to add up to a sense of being watched over, taken care of, in harmony with the universe, whatever you want to call it.

For some reason I had started out my first trip years ago wearing a pair of vinyl gloves. Soon enough, on this hot day, I understood why vinyl isn't very suitable: each hand felt as if it were encased in a little black oven. Clammy and uncomfortable, my hands squishing around in their own sweat, I longed for a pair of thin leather gloves that would breathe the same air I did. But the only place I'd find such gloves that would fit my skinny hands would probably be a fashionable women's clothing shop, and I was riding through farm country somewhere in the middle of New York.

As problems go, this was certainly a minor one. But since it was the *only* problem, I made the most of it. As the miles passed and the sun grew hotter, I became more annoyed with my lack of foresight. I didn't want to ride without gloves anymore than I'd ride without a helmet; I longed for the kind of gloves I should have bought in the first place.

Then like an oasis appearing out of the desert, a cluster of stores shimmered up ahead. And of those half a dozen stores, what to my wondering eyes should appear but — yes — a fashionable women's clothing store, with my gloves waiting for me inside. Riding away a few minutes later, I had the distinct impression that the store disappeared as soon as I was out of sight.

Same trip, next day. I suddenly realized I'd forgotten to pack a spare set of plugs. Not that I'd need them, I supposed, but still- the prepared biker carries such things, and being at times a real "what-if-er," I began to brood on having forgotten. Now, years later, I can't remember ever having to replace plugs other than at tune-up time, but then I didn't know that and pictured myself marooned in some deserted campsite for lack of a sparking plug. Bikers make great brooders — the lonely road and all that. What I needed was an auto supply store.

And the universe, as if to allay my anxiety on this first trip, murmuring "There, there now," produced said store at once. Again, a couple of shops in an area of nothing but fields and farms appeared; of the two shops, one was, of course, an auto supply store. Little boxes safely stowed away, I rode on happily, ready for anything.

Same trip, at a gorgeous crossroads in the mountains of Vermont: hills and haze and sun and shadows that had me off my bike and drooling for a photo. If only I could sit on the bike here by this route sign and put myself into that incredible landscape. But I'd have to be content with what seemed like sort of an empty shot of the bike alone. I don't know why it seemed so important to me to be in that picture or why I felt so sad that I couldn't.

I was just standing there looking off into the distance when from nowhere a car appeared beside me with two friendly looking men in it. "Hi! Are you lost? Need some help?" "No, I'm not lost ... but, say, would you take a picture for me?" One of them got out of the car with a smile, took the photo, wished me good luck on my trip, and they drove away. I felt happy out of all proportion to what had happened.

At a campsite by a mountain lake in Maine, I was rigging a plastic tarp as a fly for my tent. I'd ridden some distance into town to buy supplies, and now I found I'd forgotten to buy any cord to tie the tarp down with. Curses! I didn't want to ride back into town again. What to do? I squatted there, frowning at the tarp, when suddenly I noticed in the grass right beside me a piece of cord just the right length to cut in half and tie down two corners.

All right! I did that, but then walked over to the other side of the tent, realizing that I didn't have any cord for that side. Or rather I didn't have any until I looked down at the grass by my feet and saw the second piece, identical to the first, lying there waiting for me. A slight chill went down my spine as I looked at that piece of cord, then looked around in all directions, then vaguely skyward as I mumbled a sort of "thank you" out loud to whatever powers might be listening.

That first camping trip, alone through New England and Canada less than a year after I'd started riding, felt like the most important thing I'd ever done. It was, literally, a "new cycle" in my life, and whatever it was I was proving to myself was accomplished in those three weeks. There have been other trips, but there was only one first trip, and the rightness of everything about it was overwhelming.

And yet in such a major undertaking, it was the little events that seemed miraculous to me. I had wished for trivial things, but they loomed so large in my mind that when they were granted, I was thunderstruck. Synchronicity or whatever it is, I can't make it happen, nor would it even occur to me to try. But when it does, I go with the flow, and am grateful.

Rider October 1981

Lessons Learned

It was L. L. Bean country, up around Freeport, Maine, and I was on my maiden voyage, if one can be deemed a maiden at age 40. The day had been gray, still, foggy. That morning the ground and my tent had been completely dry, and I remembered something my grandfather had said years ago: "In the morning no dew; afternoon wet through."

I had felt very subdued all day with a lot of mild anxiety. Oh, I had a rainsuit though I'd never yet used it, and around home all I'd ever encountered was a mild shower once in a while. But now I was hundreds of miles away and in an agony of indecision for the first time. Motels weren't my notion of camping, yet the thought of setting up in the rain, being confined to my tent, and possibly rained-in the next day added to my anxiety. "Two-man" tent translated into just barely one woman plus gear — not very luxurious surroundings in which to spend a rainy day.

So all afternoon as I headed north toward Canada and the St. Lawrence, my idea being to follow that mighty river west again, I glanced uneasily at each motel I passed, feeling somehow guilty, disloyal. This was supposed to be a *camping* trip; I wanted to be able to accept compliments about my toughness, my courage, when I got back home. A motel would mess up my Wonder Woman image. Between side glances at the motels, I got a crick in my neck from checking out the darkening clouds behind, beside, and ahead. I really hadn't believed that it would actually rain on this trip. Green and golden days, clear and sparkling nights were more what I had in mind.

Finally, passing through the next town, I saw a sign pointing to a state park and asked a woman standing nearby if it was a nice place. She said oh yes, I should definitely go there, it was so beautiful, etc. So I started down that road. And a few drops of rain hit my windshield.

One thing I eventually learned about New England was that road signs often just pointed you in the right direction; they did not bother to tell you how far you might have to go to get there. So did I stop and sensibly put on my virginal rain gear, pristine in its bright yellow newness, packed conveniently right on top in my saddlebag? No. "It's just up the road," I told myself, riding on and on, and on and on.

It was raining harder when finally, with great relief, I saw the sign and the little booth at the entrance to the park. I was already envisioning myself, rugged camper of four whole days' experience, curled up in my sleeping bag with my friendly red tent between me and that lowering gray sky. The fact that the pleasant young man in charge was telling me that he was sorry, but no camping was allowed in the park, took a while to penetrate.

Disappointed and apprehensive way out of proportion to the situation (this was my first trip, remember), I rode back up that long, empty, and wetter by-the-minute road I'd just come down. And the rain was also coming down the same road, and hard. I'd head back through that town again, find a motel. No point in putting on my rainsuit now.

I was drenched, my glorious, lustrous maroon leather suit a dark, soggy mess. Took off my goggles. Bare eyes getting blitzed by the rain, but I couldn't see either way. Back to town. Where was that motel?

Stop at a gas station: "Motel's about a mile down the road." Back into the rain, squinting, flinching, crouching down behind the windshield. Ah, there it is! Oh, I see. No vacancy. But the nice lady behind the desk will call the next motel down the road; they'll hold a room for me.

Ready to leave, tension and fatigue building up, I rub a hand across my face. And so for the next five minutes the nice lady and I crawl on the floor with a flashlight looking for the contact lens which I've just flicked out of my eye. Water drips from my pigtails, from my suit, from my boots. She finds the lens, hands it to me, and picks up a mop while I plunge on out into the deluge.

Blinded by the continuing rain, missing the first crossing over the divided highway, I make the five-minute ride last 15 minutes, and when I get there, this not-so-nice lady has given my room away; she thought I wasn't coming.

But hold on — a deja vu experience occurs. She will call the next motel down the road. They will hold a room for me. This time I do not get lost; I do not make any wrong turns; they do not give my room away. Home at last, more or less. My waterproof pack turns out not to have been waterproof; I hang up all my worldly goods to drip dry at the Eagle Motel. It spreads its comforting wings over me, and I am content.

I've frequently said that I hope I live to be 120. For one thing, that way I won't even be middle-aged till I'm 60. For another, I seem to be such a late bloomer (a euphemism for slow learner) that I may need that much time to get things squared away. Lesson number one, learned on that first trip, was that I now put on my rainsuit at the first hint of rain. Amazing how much anxiety can be relieved by being prepared before the downpour when, inevitably, there's no possible place to pull off the road to suit up.

And lesson number two: If it's raining that hard, it'll probably pass within an hour, so try to find a place to sit it out, and don't keep riding in it, dummy!

Rider November 1981

Visions of a First Rally

Cruising at 75 mph seemed to be the way to go down here in good ole boy country. The highway patrol must have been patrolling the byways because they sure hadn't been in sight for a long time, and soon a flashy billboard proclaimed that we were near the exit for Loretta Lynn's Dude Ranch outside Nashville.

But where were all the bikes? I'd been wondering that all morning as my friend Dan and I headed south through the heat and haze. Somehow I'd pictured the roads for hundreds of miles in all directions solid with motorcycles: pilgrims toward Mecca, hippies toward Woodstock. And then, finally, swooping off Route 40 and onto the six miles of winding road that led to the rally site, we suddenly became part of the caravan I'd been imagining: apparently every BMW in the world was on its way to Loretta's place.

A brief stop in the shady heat of the well-organized chaos in the registration tent miraculously produced our rally packet, evidence that the U.S. mails had indeed conveyed my $15 to the right person and place many weeks before. A patch, a pin, a schedule, a garbage bag, and a shopping guide to all area stores where the bikers could drop their megabucks were among the goodies provided. We were wristbanded with one of those hospital-type plastic bracelets and told to just wave our arm as we rode in and out during the weekend.

Extricating our mounts from the swarming mass around the tent, we rode up the little hill toward the campsites. And what we saw from the top of that hill was — well — almost indescribable. Almost.

Imagine a combination of the Ringling Brothers Circus and Speed Week at Daytona moved out into the country: huge tents, concessions, displays, people — all a swirl of color and confusion — and *motorcycles* shimmering in the heat everywhere we looked. And they were all the same kind. Unreal.

We followed the gestures of those obviously in charge and headed toward the trees down at the bottom of the gentle hill. The first camping area we came to was marked "Party All Night."

...The WW II sidecar rig with the machine gun,
great for discouraging tailgaters...

Nope, that wasn't it. Farther on into the trees alongside the river we rode through "Party Half the Night." Nope, that wasn't it either. Finally we arrived at "Quiet Camping" and staked out a little homesite, grateful for at least the illusion of coolness the river provided.

For the next two days I wandered around the grounds with my camera, but the scene was so overwhelming that I scarcely knew where to begin. Should I photograph the WW II sidecar rig with the machine gun, great for discouraging tailgaters? Should I take pictures after the brief thunderstorm turned the campsite road into motocross madness with spectators gathered at the worst mud holes to watch the big bikes slosh and slide and skitter through? Or of the guy who rode his 800cc on/off road bike right into the river and was rewarded with a chorus of "For He's a Jolly Good Fellow" by the bikers already submerged in more appropriate attire?

Or of the field events like sidecar slalom and the two-up balloon toss — or of the oldest bike and the oldest rider — or the tech seminars or the safety seminars (with Stuart Munro) — or the sidecar rig with father, mother, daughter, and dog — or the incredibly weathered and battered bike from Australia with a kangaroo skin draped across what was left of the fairing after a crash somewhere in a round-the-world trip ....

Or can you imagine some poor guy, driving his car under the influence at 2 a.m. some Saturday night, trying to explain to the officer on the scene as his car is pulled from the ditch that he had just been passed by a six-foot blue teddy bear riding a motorcycle? Well, I saw one, and I don't even drink!

Horizon to horizon motorcycles — the soft puttering sound of thousands of my favorite bikes endlessly coming and going meeting people at the *Rider* booth the bike talk on every side — Mecca, Woodstock, or somewhere in between, it was the epitome of devotion to motorcycles for those nice folks who'd come from all over the country. And as the winning contestants on those old-time talent shows always used to say, "I'd sure like to thank everybody who made this possible!" See you next year.

Rider December 1981

Underneath The Arches

Almost as soon as I'd unpacked and set up camp, a neighboring camper came bustling over. "Here," he offered, opening a small square metal thing attached to two long handles. "Have a hobo pie."

I had no idea what a hobo pie was, but soon found out that this one contained fruit filling between two pieces of bread, toasted over a campfire in a metal grill. It was delicious: hot and sticky-sweet, just right with the cup of coffee that soon followed by my friendly neighbor's fire.

Hobo pie. When I was a kid, hobos used to wander down our country road and stop at our house. It was probably marked with a cryptic sign on a tree or phone pole that only another hobo would notice and understand. My mother would give them bacon and eggs, coffee, and 50 cents. Imagine living a life like that, I had thought. The freedom, the mystery of it — all your possessions in a bag over your shoulder. Where did they come from? Where were they going?

I think something of the hobo mystique lives in the touring motorcyclist. The mode of transportation we've chosen seems to some as primitive and disreputable as jumping a boxcar, the journey itself as vague and mysterious as the hobo's wanderings. We inhabit a realm fraught with danger and discomfort, both real and imaginary; for the most part we are what and where we have chosen to be.

As perceived by the average tourist, we are permanently astride our bikes, our worldly goods tied on ahead and behind, seeking the adventure they prefer to avoid, avoiding the responsibilities they must go back to, exposed to the elements, sleeping under the stars, determined gaze fixed on the ever-receding horizon. As perceived by ourselves, we are only who we are, feeling anxiety, fatigue, excitement, joy and maybe even amazement at our own courage, even if only for a week or two.

To the motoring public who may sometimes unconsciously divide all bikers into two categories — Hell's Angels and motorcycle cops — the touring rider, outfitted for days or weeks on the road, is obviously neither of those. And so everything I always wanted to know about being a vagabond but was afraid to ask, people now ask me, as if somehow that brief life on the highways each summer qualifies me — all of us — as brave, mysterious, irresponsible, slightly suspect, yet somehow glorified Residents of the Road.

Probably the one situation on a trip that puts me most in mind of the hobos of yesteryear is sitting under a bridge in the rain. Reaching the shelter of the bridge after riding through a blinding rainstorm is as great a relief as coming home when you've been away. You slither to a stop cursing your wet brakes, unsquint your eyes, let the knots untie themselves from your shoulder muscles, park the bike on the slant of the roadside the best you can, climb off, and settle in for a while.

Maybe there's a guard rail to sit on, maybe a concrete or dirt slope. Maybe there's so much water running down from everywhere you've got to just stand there or sit back on the bike again, which is itself standing in a little fast-running stream. Maybe you climb clear up to the top of the slope, sweep away the ancient artifacts (cigarette packs, candy bar wrappers, beer cans), evidence of occupation by other primitive wanderers, and perch there under the bridge as your temporary dwelling shudders and trembles around you.

Huge trucks roar through like freight trains, water hissing loudly under their wheels and flying up in ragged dirty gray curtains of spray. Rainbows of oil swirl in the centers of the lanes; they would be beautiful if they were not also lethal. The pillar you're leaning against in this Romanesque temple to engineering know-how sends deep vibrations through your whole body as it flexes massively under the tons of traffic it was designed to hold. Could this bridge ever fall, you wonder rather indifferently, knowing that it could, knowing that you're going to stay anyhow until the rain lets up.

You're glad you're here, but you also wish you weren't. It's better than out there, but it's one of the world's lonely places. You try to be patient, but the time passes with tormenting slowness. Not that you've really got to get to any special place before any particular hour, but you just want to be riding. Sweating in your rainsuit or shivering in the chill, skin crawling with impatience, you lean back with a sigh and watch the cars go by and the rain bounce endlessly on the pavement. You feel sad and a little angry: the road is going on without you.

But the motorists, turning dim, rain-blurred faces toward you as they pass, see only what you hope they will see: the brave wanderling waiting out the storm, the exotic vagabond with the patience of a reluctant Buddha meditating on the meaning of nature, in touch with the world in a way they can never be.

And finally, neither thinking nor not thinking, you simply wait.

Rider January 1982

Elixir for an Octogenarian

The gravel shifted and rolled under my wheels; my bike wallowed through as if in turbulent water. I thought fleetingly, wistfully of my old TM125 Suzuki that would have skimmed over the top of this stuff like a dragonfly over a pond. The great motorcycle journalist in search of a story. Some story it'd be if I lost it on the way down this hill, sliding upside down into the family reunion that was my destination.

Our local paper had featured an article on a man who'd ridden up from Florida to be a part of this gathering. In itself, that was nothing unusual. But only the thought that he had preceded me down this tricky road to the family campsite made me tackle the

His bright blue eyes and white hair, his stocky body and spry step...

ride instead of parking the bike and walking. Del Matthews, you see, was 85 years old.

"Well," he said as we shook hands at the pavilion beside the pond where several dozen of his relatives from all over the country were enjoying the summer evening, "if I'd known that road was so bad, I never would have ridden down it! Pretty scary. I didn't ride back up, I can tell you. I rode around through the cornfields instead, although that turned out to be just about as bad. Parked the bike up at the house this time."

Del, who had sold farm machinery and gardening supplies before he'd retired, had been here about a month earlier, then left for a trip around the state to visit old friends, returning now for the reunion. When I realized that he'd left his bike a half mile away, I also realized I'd have to ride back there to get some photos. When faced with the choice between the cornfields and the gravel road, I chose the road and zipped back up with considerably more style and less anxiety now that I had an audience. Following me in a car, Del disappeared briefly, then reappeared from one of the big barns, helmeted, astride his new red Honda CM400A complete with fairing and bags.

After our photo session, we rejoined the picnic and sat down to talk. He didn't bother to put on the glasses that stuck out of his shirt pocket to read a few paragraphs in the copy of *Rider* that I'd brought to show him. His bright blue eyes and white hair, his stocky body and spry step, his easy laugh and his supply of anecdotes all added up to one very amiable and interesting gentleman.

"My wife had died," he explained, "and to deal with all the grief and loneliness I was driving all over in my car to visit friends and relatives. Seventeen thousand miles in one year — a lot of gas money and not much adventure."

So, influenced by one of his younger cronies, a mere stripling of 81 who'd been riding for some time, and remembering the excitement of riding his Pierce Arrow back when he was 18, Del walked into the dealer's one day. "Will you sell an 85-year-old man a motorcycle?" The bike was delivered the next day, Friday the 13th, a date that might have proved significant considering the dealer provided him with no lessons whatsoever.

But carefully, in his yard and around his neighborhood, Del taught himself how to ride — or remembered. And on the second day of his rebirth as a motorcyclist he headed out on a hundred-mile trip to visit his son.

We all shudder to think of tall, strong teenage boys with the quick reflexes of youth, setting out on motorcycles with no instructions and a macho image to live up to. What about an arthritic 85year-old man whose feet just touch the ground, whose experience consisted of a year's riding 67 years ago?

On that first trip, the inevitable tipover occurred at a stop sign where the pavement sloped away from under his foot. "The guy in the car behind me jumped out and helped me pick up the bike. I wasn't hurt, only embarrassed."

Later, on a short trip with his old friend, Del swung too wide on a lefthander, caught a road sign pole with his crash bar, and went down. As his octogenarian buddy helped him get up, he also delivered a lecture about Del's ever undertaking a long trip up north. "You'll never make it," he scolded. "You're too old for this!"

And the worst of the falls, in his second week of riding, came when he tried to avoid some gravel in the road. "The bike went sliding down the road and I went sliding after it," Del recounted with a wry grin. "I knew I should get right back on, just like when you fall off a horse. And I haven't fallen down since."

"And you know," he continued, digging into the plate of potato salad and baked beans, "the best part is that my arthritis hardly bothers me anymore. Riding the motorcycle keeps me limber — all the getting on and off, pushing it around. I stop every hour when I ride, do some exercises. I'm in better shape than I've been in for years. Went back to work full time a while ago — building outdoor furniture."

From freeways to cornfields, he's ridden 5000 miles this year. Del Matthews, Edgewater, Florida. Born in 1896, reborn in 1981. Ride on!

Rider February 1982

Friendly Encounters

This is not another ride-in-the-rain story although it starts out with one. This is a nice-people story. Motorcycle literature is filled with horror stories and accounts of hostility that we all seem compelled to share every time we get together. I've tried to do my share of the sharing, but the truth is (and I almost blush to admit it, as if somehow I haven't lived up to the biker's image) that I hardly have any horror stories to tell. Maybe, like appearing on the cover of *Sports Illustrated* seems to jinx some athletes, this column will result in a reversal of my good fortune, but (knock on wood) here goes.

A while back, my friend Dan and I were on a short Sunday afternoon ride, only 15 miles or so between us and our destination. A fair number of dark clouds were rushing around through the already overcast sky, but we figured the rain would either hold off or miss us. Wrong! With a suddenness that gave us no time to get to any kind of shelter, the first few huge drops turned into an all-out rainstorm. Nothing to do but pull over right where we were.

And where we were was the edge of someone's front lawn. A few evergreens gave scant protection from the deluge. We inched off the road and onto the spongy grass that was already several inches deep in puddles and just sat there on the bikes to wait it out, leather jackets soaking up the water, jeans and boots already saturated. Not a very pleasant interlude on a Sunday afternoon.

But then through the uproar of the wind and rain, our helmets still on, we became aware of what sounded like a woman's voice calling to us. Or was she hollering at us to get off her property? I wouldn't have been surprised — bikers, you know. Bad types.

Dan sloshed a little closer to the front door where she stood making gestures. "She wants us to put our bikes around back, in the barn," he called as he hurried back. And so we did, making our way with difficulty back onto the road, around the corner, into her driveway, and finally into the open barn. With relief we took off our helmets and sat down to wait in comfort.

A while later, as the storm swept off on its way to torment any other unfortunate riders it could find, Dan pushed the bikes out into the puddle-filled drive while I went to the back door to thank her. "Come in, come in!" she called. "I've made some coffee for you." She appeared carrying a tray out onto the enclosed porch. I turned back to Dan. "She wants us to have coffee with her," I announced with surprise and pleasure. And so we did. And an amiable talk besides. Although the sun never came back out that day, we could hardly tell the difference. The brightness of that encounter stayed with us.

There were others, like the old couple who had driven behind us for a long time up in New England. When we all happened to stop at the same place for an ice-cream cone, they came bustling over to tell us how impressed they were with the precise and careful way in which we rode, and added that's the way everyone should ride.

There was the French woman who managed the cabin site up along the St. Lawrence River, coming to my cabin on a cold night to bring me, unasked, a hot plate so I could make coffee and with it a tiny glass of cognac (teetotaler though I am).

There was also the German woman who ran a restaurant in the mountains of eastern Pennsylvania, coming outside to greet us and admire our German bikes, and bringing paper towels to wipe our windshields when we left.

Other vignettes: The people camping nearby who gave me newspapers to help me get my fire started on a wet evening. The motel owner who brought me a big plastic cover for my bike because she'd heard over the radio that heavy rain and hail were predicted. The campground owner in a heavily touristed part of the Adirondack Mountains who spoke pleasantly to me in a restaurant and invited me to camp as her guest. The dozen German tourists in a rest area who didn't speak English but wished me well anyhow. The park manager and his wife in the campground in Nova Scotia who invited me to share their picnic supper. The doctor in the hospital in Maine who made a special trip on a Saturday to check my eye, which had been causing me trouble from what I feared was a corneal abrasion under my contact lens (it wasn't) and invited me to stay with her and her husband if I didn't feel like riding. The half-dozen occupants of a tiny cabin-like restaurant on Route 9 in Maine who watched me pull in, dismount, take off my rainsuit and enter, greeting me as warmly as if they'd been waiting for me. And — small world — one of the women, it turned out, had a sister who lived about 10 miles up the road from me.

The park ranger in Vermont who drove up to my rather isolated campsite in the state park to see if I needed anything before it got dark. The man and woman in the pickup truck who honked wildly at me to let me know that my pack (which I'd forgotten to bungee back up when I'd stopped to get something out of it) was bouncing down the highway behind me, and who drove me back to get it when I'd parked my bike and started to jog back for it. The guy in the car behind me who slowed down when my rain pants blew out of a carelessly left open saddlebag, opened his door, picked them up off the road without even stopping, handed them to his passenger who handed them to me as the car went by.

And although it doesn't exactly belong in this list of friendly encounters with other human beings, I can't leave out the pop machine at that glorious campsite on the coast of Nova Scotia that accepted my 30 cents, tossed the can of pop clear out of its mysterious opening to land at my feet, and gave me back 25 cents change!

I mean, maybe I do have some horror stories of my own to tell, but I just seem to have forgotten most of them. A curious brightness reduces them to faint, small shadows as the luminous landscape that is all my trips spreads out and rolls away over all the roads behind me.

Rider March 1982

....The bell-like chiming of the rigging clanging against the masts of the moored boats.

Sounds to Sleep and Wake by

A long time ago I did a column on bike sounds, but every trip has a whole symphony of other kinds of sounds that play like background music as I travel, creating moods and memories.

On my first-ever trip, I camped in late afternoon in a secluded spot that the two young sons of the campground owner showed me: their favorite spot by a small stream running rapidly over large stones, making an endless, flute-like cadenza that followed me melodiously into sleep that first night out on the road alone.

In many campsites, the peculiar noise of a light breeze at night in the trees above my tent has sounded like rain, and I am momentarily dismayed as I imagine having to pack up and ride in the rain, come morning. But then I look out and see the stars and am momentarily puzzled until I realize the source of sound.

And sometimes, of course, it *is* rain I hear on the tent, but finally I learned to let it put me to sleep, like the pleasant ticking of a soft clock. No amount of agonizing over the prospect of rain is going to make it stop falling, so I might as well relax and let it lull me instead of trouble me. My tent is secure; the seams are tight. I will worry about the rain tomorrow, if indeed it's still raining.

When I camp somewhere under pines, there is the little dry touch of the falling needles as they hit the slanted roof of my tent, and the tiny scratchy whisper of their slide to the ground. And always, but *always* in the middle of the night is the rustle of some small creature about its nocturnal business in the grass mere inches away from my staring but unseeing eyes.

Once, however, the rustle was much too loud for comfort, and easing the tent zipper open, I aimed my flashlight in the direction of the sound. There, rummaging in a nearly empty bag of french fries that I'd completely forgotten about and carelessly left at the base of a nearby tree, was a huge skunk. I clicked off the light and lay down, grateful our paths hadn't crossed and that I'd had an unriled skunk teach me about disposing of food rather than a hungry bear. I hate to think what devastation a candy bar forgotten in a pants pocket might have caused, or a loaf of bread left in a saddlebag.

Sometimes the nicest sensation on a bike trip has been the *lack* of sound — or at least of a certain kind of sound. The difficult ride down that deep sandy road in Michigan was well worth the anxiety when later, stretched out in my sleeping bag with a good book and my flashlight to read by, I became aware that there was no sound of traffic — not the faintest — not from anywhere. It's hard to find a regular campground that you can take a big bike into and be far enough away from any roads to escape that distant hum, the occasional whine of gears as a trucker climbs a long hill somewhere. I shut the book, turned out the light, and just listened to the silence for a while before I slept.

The opposite kind of campground is unavoidable once in a while, and one night after a gray, uncomfortably cold, misty day on the roads in Maine, I pulled into a park crowded with the usual combination of RVs and tents. Friendly place — too friendly, I thought, for parties seemed to be going on all around me that evening — not my style of camping at all. But as I wiggled down into my sleeping bag, warm at last, the rise and fall of voices on all sides seemed pleasant and comforting rather than annoying. I drifted off into my best sleep of the trip as the disembodied laughter and conversation filtered through my red walls. "Just folks," I thought drowsily. "Just folks ... havin' ... a good ... time …."

The happiest part of a number of trips has been a visit with my younger son, a sailboat builder ever since high school. North

Carolina, New Hampshire, Maryland — I ride along the edges of the ocean to wherever he is and camp on the shore for my brief stay. He is always off to somewhere and so am I: he on water, I on land. Our visits are affectionate and always too short. The motorcycle seems alien and small in the marina parking lot as I exchange my leather boots for deck shoes. And the lovely sound that always accompanies these visits is the bell-like chiming of the rigging clanging against the masts of the moored boats. I sleep and wake to it. It blends in with the sound of my bike as I ride away and becomes part of the whole symphony.

I suppose those things we *see* on our trips provide our most vivid memories. But underlying all the sights, our awareness turned down too low to hear it most of the time, is a kind of subliminal concert of sound. To be sure, the sound of the bike is the sweetest sound of all. But the next time you turn it off, listen to what starts up all around you. The trip takes on a new dimension when we let ourselves go beyond what our eyes can see.

Rider April 1982

Moods

Time and place: A splendid summer afternoon in Nova Scotia as I headed for my eventual goal, the spectacular Cabot Trail around Highlands National Park. By rights I should have been very happy, especially with so many foggy, rainy days behind me along with six hours of seasickness earlier on the "Bluenose," the ferry from Bar Harbor to Yarmouth. But no. I rode along thinking of only one thing: Where am I going to camp tonight?

I glanced at the scenery with annoyance. What right had it to be so beautiful when 1 was so irritable? I was also annoyed with myself for letting myself feel that way. But riding alone seems to cause an intense inward focus that can be either pleasant or unpleasant, depending on what it reveals. And for some reason even the lovely rolling hills couldn't lift me for an hour or so till 1 found a place to camp.

One of the curious things I've had to learn to deal with in touring has been what I've found to be the incredible array of moods to be experienced all within the same day on the road, changing hour by hour, the peaks and valleys of the scenery more than matched by my own ups and downs. I would have thought that merely riding through gorgeous landscapes would put me in a good mood, or that rain or mechanical trouble or tedious terrain would be instant downers. Not so.

I've learned that moods can rise and fall in an almost predictable pattern when I'm on the road. Typically one anxious moment is early in the morning as I'm packing to go. "What if the bike doesn't start?" I keep wondering as I strike camp and load up. (Why wouldn't it start, for Pete's sake? And the once or twice that it hasn't started, I've managed to deal with it one way or another.)

Although I'm a habitual breakfast eater at home, I rarely eat in the morning before hitting the road: too eager to get packed, get going, get some miles in. But then, when I've ridden for a couple of hours, my early morning enthusiasm for being on the road starts to diminish rather suddenly, and I ride along feeling grumpy and depressed until I realize what the problem is: I'm hungry! So the next restaurant is my next stop. And boy, am I ready to eat then!

From breakfast through midday into late afternoon, I'm on top of the world. Prime riding hours. I speed, or I putter; I stop and look at the sights, take pictures, talk to people. Ah, this is the life!

But then, as the sun heads gradually for the horizon, I start feeling strange about those long shadows creeping over the landscape. I stop and consult my old campsite book. Doesn't look like much up ahead the way I'm going. Damn. Where will I sleep tonight? And my own shadows close in around me till I get to somewhere.

Yet sometimes on days that I *ought* to feel kind of down, nothing seems to keep me from smiling. I wrote in a trip journal once that it had been threatening rain all afternoon, but that I still felt like camping and not taking a motel. "The thunder didn't seem ominous," I wrote, "but friendly somehow, coming nearer, going away." There've been days when riding in the rain all day seemed not only acceptable but even desirable, maybe after several days of broiling sun: a slow, quiet, thoughtful time. Yet on the same trip I might respond to an overcast sky as if it were the end of the world. Who can explain it?

One night I ended up almost afloat with just my Ensolite pad between my sleeping bag and the definitely sloshy nylon floor of my tent. But I'd done all I could do at the time — moved the tent several times in the wind and rain and dark, covered half of me with a big garbage bag to keep the drips off — and I actually went happily to sleep thinking that it was a neat little adventure and glad I had learned that day what I needed to do to make both the tent and my leaky rainsuit a little more "seaworthy."

On some days something not working right on the bike feels like a challenge instead of a disaster. Or the hot, flat, straight roads of Florida seem peaceful and simple rather than tiresome and empty. It's kind of like looking at a glass of water and seeing it as either half empty or half full: all a question of viewpoint.

I'm usually happy when I'm out on the road; I am, after all, where I've chosen to be. But especially when I tour alone, I'm acutely aware of the shifts in mood throughout a day. They've been easier to deal with once I learned that they usually accompany me: the gray worries that throw shadows on even the brightest landscape, or the curious little smile that outlasts the rain clouds gathering along the dark horizon.

Rider May 1982

First Ride

I had thought I was safe: I lived 40 miles on one side of Cleveland, he, 40 miles on the other — a student at the university where I had my first teaching job, always pestering me to go for a ride on his motorcycle.

Motorcycle? Me? No way. I seemed vaguely aware that nice folks drove cars while — well — other people, certain less acceptable people, rode motorcycles. The following year I was teaching elsewhere, so the student and his invitation were the farthest things from my mind.

Until one day that summer, that is, when he suddenly appeared in my yard ("Hi! Just happened to be passing through!") astride what I must admit did seem to me even then like a really beautiful BSA 650 — turquoise! — and he "just happened to have" two helmets, and it *was* a gorgeous day. The bike shone in the sun, alien and totally intriguing. I hesitated for a long time — three or four seconds — and said OK.

We rode long and gently through that summer afternoon and stopped after several hours at a rather elegant place to eat. To walk into a place like that, carrying my helmet — I felt so cool! That helmet marked me, or so I supposed, as an incredibly adventurous human being, to be gazed at and admired by all. (It took, in fact, several years of riding on my own bike years later before I was willing to leave my helmet behind when I got off. Even the inconvenience of carrying it and a jacket and half a dozen packages wasn't enough to make me lock it on the bike. No one would know I rode a motorcycle!)

After a pleasant dinner, I was returned gently and safely to my house, my whole way of thinking about bikes and bikers completely changed. And a few years later — well, you know the story: my first lesson on friend Dan's BMW, my first bike (a GT250 Suzuki), motocross (TM125 Suzuki), road racing (RD250 Yamaha), a 600 BMW, and since '75 my beloved white R90/6.

But there's one key word in that story of my first ride, and without it there might have been no second ride. That word is "gently." We've all known people who see what we arrive at work on and exclaim in horror, "You'd never get me on one of those things again! My next door neighbor's brother-in-law took me for a ride once and I was never so scared in my life! Why, he went 100 mph down that road, and I .... " No need to go on. What happens to us on that first ride may determine whether we ever ride again or not.

For some, a motorcycle can seem as exotic, dangerous, and disreputable a form of transportation as a tightwire over Niagara Falls. And if our first ride resembles the old Indy races when the mechanic rode with the driver and was subject to all the same dangers — if we return from that first ride with the notion that all motorcycles are *supposed* to be ridden at maximum speed and at terrifying angles, we may indeed choose never to go again — particularly women (perhaps) who typically don't spend their adolescent years crouched behind the wheel of a careening car with buddies to impress and a macho image to live up to.

I was lucky. My first ride was with someone who took every precaution to make me feel safe and relaxed. My second ride, years later with Dan, was especially reassuring. He explained all his moves: his lane positions, his decisions to pass or not pass, his speeding up or slowing down. From the first day Dan had me as a passenger, he seemed to assume that I would want to learn all I could about riding, and sure enough, a month later I had a bike of my own.

I guess the moral of this story is that when we have a chance to give someone that never-to-be forgotten first ride, we shouldn't try to impress our probably nervous passenger with how similar to Kenny Roberts' our own cornering technique is or how great the bike handles at 120 mph down the freeway at night in the rain. We'll make more converts to riding with a gentle first trip that leaves them hungry for more than with a gut-wrenching, boot-scraping, heart-stopping ride that provides them with all the wrong answers to everything they always wanted to know about motorcycling but were afraid to ask.

Rider June 1982

Cycle Song

When the roar comes
through the green summer,
it is you, coming in thunder.

I listen you along the afternoon road,
the sound in my head pulling you closer.

My eyes, closed, remember your wrists at ease
with the lightning under your hands;
the angle of your thighs eloquent,
your body speaks casual commands.

On behind you
I feel the horizons move back;
people move back and touch us
only with their eyes.

My life is at stake.
I am kept safe by the sinews
of your wrists, your fingers,
by the long hard muscles of your thighs,
by the balance that delicately moves
somewhere deep within your blood.

If there are tapestries still to be made,
one will show us with many silver threads
the color of chrome,

and the richness of the world
behind us in browns and greens.

Scarlet will mark the magic spot
where you have slain
my own invisible dragons
and carried me away.

The wild deep sound can be woven
only as golden images:
stars perhaps shattered,
falling on our shoulders;
or the sun sliding under our wheels
and lying like a deep rug
over all the land.

from *Rumors of Ecstasy — Rumors of Death*
Barntwood Press 1981

Almost Never

People who know me well are aware that one thing I'm fond of saying when I wax philosophic is that words like "always" and "never" simply don't work where human beings are concerned. I frequently catch myself just as I'm about to let slip one of those no-nos and modify what I was about to say.

And even though I've seen myself often enough do a 180-degree turn in attitude as life goes along, there was *one* experience I'd have bet you a million dollars that I'd never have. If someone had ever told me that this country girl from just outside a small town in Ohio, Miss Cautious Rider of All Time, would suddenly find herself lane splitting on the Los Angeles freeways during morning rush hour, I'd have responded with an incredulous stare and the most scathing putdown I could think of for such an unimaginable failure to recognize my superior intelligence and motorcycling savvy. In fact, when I glanced at Rich Cox's article, "Riding the Line" *(Rider,* August '81) I snorted a "Hmmph!" of disdain and flipped the page in search of something worth my time. Well, I just looked up Rich's story to see if I'd done it right. I must have — I'm here to tell about it.

On the last night of the *Rider* road test weekend we were still a hundred miles or so away from "home" — my motel in Thousand Oaks, and the other riders' actual homes. It was late; we were tired. Dorde Woodruff's dad lived only 20 minutes away from where we'd stopped for a last meal; she and I both were way over the comfort limit with our contact lenses. So Dorde called and told her dad we would be staying there for the night — a welcome decision that necessitated our riding the last miles of the trip back to the *Rider* offices the next morning before the traffic got heavy on the freeway.

Later Dorde would say to me, "Well, it just never occurred to me to tell you what we'd do if we got stuck in traffic. I never thought it'd bother you — you've raced and everything." Boy, have I learned that that phrase covers a multitude of evils I'm supposed to be able to cope with!

Although we'd gotten off to a little later start than we'd planned, we were zipping along just fine, and I was wishing I'd had a chance to ride all the test bikes a second time, for now I was seeing some things about the Suzuki that I hadn't noticed before. I was also wondering how anyone tests suspensions out in California; the roads seem to have scarcely a ripple in them. The seams in the concrete freeway slabs were giving the bike more of a workout than it'd had during the whole weekend. Maybe *Rider* could ship all test bikes to northern Ohio for suspension tests; all the roads around here look like the aftermath of a WWII bombing raid.

Concentrating on following Dorde, I began to notice the traffic becoming heavier and slower. And eventually, glancing ahead, I saw what seemed to be a solid mass of cars stretching to the horizon. It never occurred to me what was going to happen. I simply shifted gears, both literally and figuratively, and resigned myself to a long term of stop and go, feet-up-feet-down riding. That's the way you do it around here.

But no, Dorde just flicked the little Kaw in between the two lines of barely creeping cars and continued traveling steadily forward. To try to describe my state of shock and horror is impossible. "Oh no! No!" I yelled, beeping my horn and shaking my head wildly. Surely this was not happening. Real people didn't do this, only Hell's Angels and Kamikaze pilots in old war films. She just rode on.

I watched in terror, waiting for the inevitable: Dorde would die right in front of me, crushed to death by two maniacal drivers who would, with gestures, plot to "get her" as soon as they became aware of her presence. And I'd be next, pinned between two furiously opened doors by irate motorists who would rather kill bikers than go to work.

This went against every instinct I'd developed in all my years of riding. Back and forth over the slippery round white lane markers I went, dodging a rear fender here, a big mirror there. Through this solid wall of flashing brakelights she rode as if it were nothing more than a neon-lit back alley.

Eventually I came out of shock enough to realize that many other bikers were also threading their way through these narrow pathways.

Suddenly there was a biker right behind me, gesturing to something on the back of my bike. Thank God, something was wrong with the Suzuki and I'd have to pull over. I honked and gestured to Dorde, and we stopped on the inside lane up against the divider wall. It was my pack coming loose; I re-bungeed it and asked Dorde (hoping I didn't sound quite as terror-stricken as I felt), "Do we *have* to keep doing this?"

That's when she countered with her comment on my having raced, and also thought to inform me that what we were doing was not illegal, "It's not? It sure is at home!" (I should have read Rich's article!) "Well — OK." And on we went.

I finally quit hitting the brakes every time all the cars ahead of me did since my motorcycle did not go forward so well with both brakes on at all times. I began to see that so far not one motorist had even so much as directed a dirty look at me and that the narrow space we were traveling was more than plenty big enough to slip these small bikes through. I restored the circulation to my hands by letting up a bit in the deathgrip I had on the bars. Although my pulse rate stayed at about 246, I began to feel that I just might survive. And after only a few millennia, sure 'nuff, there we were pulling into the parking lot at *Rider*.

I felt as if I had come through the Maginot Line, the beach at Normandy, and Pork Chop Hill. Me whiteline it?

Never again ... unless ... except.... perhaps ....

Rider September 1982

Miles of Smiles

Like most writers, I collect scraps of paper, file folders, notebooks full of ideas. Some of them turn into stories, poems, columns; some never go anywhere. I have a little collection of bike material, none quite long enough for a column, but all of a kind: things I've seen or heard as a biker that made me chuckle, or at least smile a lot.

About a year ago I sat with a friend looking out a restaurant window waiting for breakfast when in rode a man on a well-cared-for Gold Wing pulling a beautiful little wooden trailer that looked like a piece of fine furniture with polished fittings. In the trailer sat a very large German Shepherd who peacefully waited outside while his master ate. Rider and faithful companion were about to embark on a trip from Ohio to New Mexico.

Another shaggy dog story happened this past summer when my friend from California, Mary Austin (whom I'd ridden with on the Rider road test — September '82 issue), called from about an hour away to ask if she and her friend might drop in to say hello; they were on a cross country trip. All right! And as I went out to greet them a little later, what to my wondering eyes should appear in addition to both riders and what looked like a moving van full of equipment piled on the Gold Wing, was Imp. A little dustmop of a dog, he had ridden from California to Nova Scotia sitting in the tank bag in front of Mary's friend, Eric. In answer to my questions, no, he didn't get restless, no, he didn't try to jump out. (That sounds as if I asked him the questions.) Anyhow, now he was on his way back to California with his personal chauffeurs. He must hold the world's sitting still record for small, fuzzy, motorcycle riding dogs.

The scene changes to my Aunt Dorothy who is 83 and lives in a beautiful retirement home on Tampa Bay in Clearwater, Florida. Always interested in what her niece is up to, she subscribed to Rider when I started writing this column. As she picks up her copy at the desk, she just smiles at the people in charge, telling them nothing. As she puts it in a recent letter, "Just to show you how increasingly weird I must appear to our mail clerks, I am not only getting Rider but am beginning to receive catalogs containing every possible piece of motorcycle equipment known to man! The people here cannot reconcile my gentle, courteous demeanor with that other, darker side of leather jackets, etc. I offer no explanation!" I just break up every time I picture my elegant, white-haired aunt clutching the latest info on turbocharging your Honda and dressing your Hawg as she smiles mysteriously and walks away.

And speaking of senior citizens, my column "Elixir for an Octogenarian" (February '82) described 85-year-old Del Matthews' ride from his Florida home to his family reunion in Ohio, returning to biking after a little layoff of 67 years! Well, he rode up again for this year's fest and has put 12,000 miles on that Honda in 15 months. Maybe I should suggest that he take a ride from Edgewater over to Tampa to visit Dorothy. Del, striding into the lobby, helmet in hand ... wouldn't *that* give the management of her place something to wonder about!

And now not a smile but a laugh that happened years ago when I was first riding. Just before a gentle summer evening's ride with my brother-in-law, I'd been reading a safe riding article on how to get your weight back and lighten the front end if hitting an obstacle in the road was inevitable. In a small town miles away just about dark, we realized we'd made a wrong turn. I made a cautious turn back the right way while Chuck, a little ahead of me, rode on over a set of railroad tracks before making his turn. Before he could rejoin me, somehow a train came ghosting along the rails and the flashers weren't working! When he finally rode up to me after a long wait on the other side, he shook his head and said, "I almost didn't see that train!" Suddenly an image from the article I'd been reading appeared in mind. "If hitting an obstacle seems inevitable," I shouted over to him as we took off, "you get your weight back ... " and that was as far as I got before collapsing over my tank with laughter at the thought of lightening the front end in order to better deal with centerpunching a moving freight train. He kept looking over and hollering, "What's so funny?" Must have taken me two miles to quit laughing and tell him.

Oh well. Maybe you had to be there.

Rider December 1982

Contributions to Safe Riding

When I was a kid, from about age 8 to maybe 14, I spent a lot of time daydreaming about being the World's Only Girl Midget Auto Racer. My Schwinn Roadmaster was my blue #5 Offenhauser, and the road that circled the neighborhood was the Indy track. I pedaled mile after furious mile, completely engrossed in my fantasy. Thousands cheered as I entered Victory Lane, the only girl ever to ....

Somehow the chance never presented itself for that particular dream to come true. But neither had I ever dreamed that I would someday ride a motorcycle, and soon after I began, see my first motocross race. Something like an old memory stirred. I had ridden horseback most of my life, and those wild bikes out there, like spooked horses, combined with my race-car-driver fantasy to create the sudden realization: I could do that!

So about six months after I had learned to ride, I bought a TM125 Suzuki and went racing. The fact that I was then 40 years old seemed of no significance. "When the pupil is ready, the teacher will appear," goes a Zen saying.

I didn't do badly, all things considered. Although I was nowhere against the men, I did race at one track where a "Powder Puff" race attracted ten to fifteen girls each month. I never took a first, but was consistently third or fourth racing against fearless 14-year-olds who didn't care if they crashed or not.

I don't think I ever got the hole-shot into that first turn, but I never DNF'd, either. And those couple of years of motocross were probably the most useful riding I ever did. The terrain over which we rode was difficult beyond imagining: ruts, mud, hills, jumps, whoop-de-doos — I've never ridden a bronc in the rodeo, but I imagine that's the only activity that would compare.

But the point of all this is to say that although I learned to ride on the street on my GT250 Suzuki, and although I was taught to pay scrupulous attention to safe riding techniques, I don't think anything could have made me a better rider more quickly than dirt-bike riding. Not that I necessarily advocate everyone's going out to race motocross; booniebashing would do just as well: pastures, fire trails, anywhere you are allowed to take an off-road bike.

In that first summer of racing I was street riding one day out in the country alone, doing about 60, when something happened that, had I not had the experience on a wildly bucking dirt bike, I doubt I would have been able to handle. I heard a funny little "pop" but didn't recognize it. And suddenly my bike was all over the road, swerving, sliding, crossing the centerline and back as if it were having convulsions. Dumbfounded, I fought it somehow to the side of the road and got it stopped, still upright. It was then that I discovered the source of the noise: a rear-wheel blowout. And soon after I'd started a long uphill push to the nearest gas station, a local resident came out to help me. I was grateful; that 250 with a flat tire weighed about a thousand pounds!

Just holding onto a bike that was behaving as crazily as that one was a job. And I don't think there's any street riding experience that could have prepared me to handle that situation the way motocross had. At that point a couple of months of dirt-bike shenanigans had possibly saved me a bad accident.

I'd started racing motocross when chronic foot trouble had just about put me out of competition in running. But after an operation corrected the problem, I quit motocross to concentrate on running again. Then during another long seige of injury I happened to see my first motorcycle road race, and a new RD250 Yamaha became my blue #5 Offenhauser! I was at it again, this time on smooth pavement at horrendous and exhilarating speeds and lean angles.

The May '82 *BMW News* had a fascinating article, *Conquering the Nurburgring* by Lt. Col. Ronald Marcum, in which he describes a three-day training session designed "to learn performance limits of both ourselves and our machines" held on that famous race course in Germany. How I would have loved to do that!

"Would have." Not now, I think. The time was right for me to race when I did. Those few years of racing — in the dirt and on the track — I think I was the best rider then that I will ever be. I hope the moves I learned will always be with me.

Rider February 1983

Gripes

Since I seem to be in a bad mood today anyhow, it occurred to me to write, for once, a crabby column. None of that poetry stuff, just gripes.

Let's see. I'm mad at the guy I saw riding last summer with no shirt and no helmet. No big deal, you say? They all do it? Yes, but not with two (2!) little kids also on the bike, one in front of him, one behind, wearing sun suits and no helmets either.

I'm mad at the guy on the bike who pulled out of a road behind me and began tailgating me horrendously as I drove my car home. I flashed my brake lights, gestured, did everything I could to back him off, picturing his unhelmeted head buried in my trunk should I have to stop suddenly. He just waved and grinned, waited for the oncoming pickup truck to get a little closer, then passed between the truck and me on the centerline. The driver of the truck looked incredulous and pale.

I'm mad because I was all packed and ready to go on one last tour late this past summer, woke up that morning, said, "I don't feel like going," and didn't. And I don't know why. Maybe the key word is "late": The summer had slipped away; the beginning of school was too close; too many preparations were as yet undone, Maybe it was that "little voice" we all seem to have telling us things we don't always listen to and should. I don't know.

I'm mad at the image that advertisers insist on perpetuating: that bikes are ridden only by macho males who wear only black leather and who seem to ride only at midnight as they are leaving all-night cafes after, no doubt, drinking for hours with their equally macho buddies.

Seems to me the advertising is all aimed at what is probably already the best established market: the young adult male. The thousands of untouched buyers of both sexes glance blankly at Darth Vader astride the newest turbocharged XX1100 Whatever plotting his midnight machinations, and turn away from the TV set or magazine page, uninterested, uninvolved. Oh, Advertisers! There are more of us out here than exist in that dark tunnel of your vision.

And with all our talk on safety, where are the white leather jackets and the red leather jackets and the yellow ones and the green ones and all the rest of the spectrum that would be so much more visible to the motorists than black and brown? Only in custom megabucks leathers, for the most part.

I'm mad because last Sunday, the first day in weeks I had some guilt-free hours in which to ride, my cold and long-unused bike stalled on the way out the driveway and didn't have enough juice left to turn that big starter over again. But what really frosts me is that BMW quit putting kick starters on their bikes in 1975. Mine is, of course, a '75.

I'm mad because I didn't see the chuckhole that bent my rim a couple of trips ago, and because I didn't keep following that road along that river in Quebec just to see where I'd end up, and because I get scared when weird people follow me and I'm aware of how vulnerable we all are on bikes.

I'm mad because I've been too paranoid to leave my bike parked somewhere and do some leisurely sightseeing just like all the rest of the tourists, or passed up a neat campsite because I couldn't chain the bike to something an arm's length away.

I'm mad because I don't ride my bike as often as I "should," whatever that means in the snowbelt of northeastern Ohio, and because when I am on the road, I always feel like I've got to hurry up and get somewhere, whether to the grocery store or to Nova Scotia.

I'm mad because sometimes I still spend time looking at the people looking at me when I should be looking at the road ahead of me, beside me, behind me. The "It's a girl!" reaction still pleases me, and I wish I'd grow up just a little more so it didn't matter so much whether anybody paid attention to me or not.

And I'm a little mad because I'm writing a column while I'm mad, always a dangerous thing. Have you ever written and sent an angry letter and then wished you hadn't? But if I sleep on it, I'll miss my deadline, and then I won't be the only one mad.

But come to think of it, now that I've dumped about 10 years' worth of gripes, I don't feel so mad anymore. Look for the next angry column in the March 1992 issue.

Rider March 1983

Fast, Faster, Fastest

I wonder if human beings are born with go-fast genes? It's never been enough to simply go someplace; eventually someone will establish a record for getting there faster, by whatever means, than anyone else has ever done.

As toddlers, we try to run almost before we've mastered walking. Next it's races on our tricycles, then bicycles, horses, cars, motorcycles. Even the Amish youth out here in the county where I live sometimes get arrested for, well, if not speeding, then reckless driving with their horses and buggies. There's always a match race brewing when a farmer has just purchased a new buggy horse fresh off an area race track.

If we're not born with the desire to go fast, then we soon acquire it, inundated as we are with advertising from all sides — especially in the motorcycling industry — assuring us that the only bike worth having is the one that goes the fastest.

Now I'd be among the first to vote "no" if the issue of the 55 mph speed limit were ever put on the ballot. When I think of the money that went into the engineering and design of our high speed freeway system years ago and now find myself creeping along the flat, straight 400 miles between Cleveland and Chicago at 55 mph, I can only shake my head.

Granted, I'll take the usual five mph over the limit that most of us feel entitled to, and maybe a couple more for good measure. But when I'm cruising along at 62 mph and suddenly see the cagily parked patrol car, the jolt I feel in my solar plexus must at least faintly resemble death in the electric chair. A life of crime is not for me. My nervous system couldn't stand it.

So mostly I don't speed. That's not to say I don't get the urge, but I'm so resigned to going more slowly that touring in Canada a few years ago took some getting used to: 70 mph felt like Mach I.

Once in a while, way out in the country, on a straight, smooth stretch of empty road, my bike will communicate to me its boredom with my conservative riding style, and in response I'll nudge it up to 80 or so for maybe a quarter mile. Its high-speed smoothness and stability make me want more, but I don't take it. I back off, not out of fear, but out of awareness that on the street there are just too many variables: the deep pothole, the unexpected pile of gravel, the debris, the animal suddenly up out of the ditch, the car out of the hidden drive. It's not worth the anxiety.

On the track it was a different story, and except for the woodchuck who now and again ambled across Turn One and an occasional migration of frogs from the swamp along the long back straightaway at Nelson Ledges, the racing environment was fairly predictable. Scraping a boot toe there felt right; it meant I'd pitched it over into that turn the way you're supposed to. But if the unpredictable did happen, trained corner workers were there in seconds to tend to a fallen rider and bike, an ambulance right behind them, and a pit hospital only half the track away.

I remember my amazement years ago before I'd ever even seen a real-life road race, let alone ridden in one, when I saw a rider whip around a traffic circle on a little-traveled road, hanging off his bike in typical road race style, inside knee flirting with the pavement. "Wow!" I thought, having seen enough pictures to understand his fantasy.

It might well be that if I divested my bike of all the stuff on it that I was griping about in another column, I might become a slightly different person, one who did indeed street ride all-out all the time. But I doubt it. There are days when I ride more aggressively than other days, corner and brake harder, nudge the limit a little more. But outside eyes would still perceive me as very cautious.

What I wish is that advertisers would back off from their focus on FAST-FASTER-FASTEST, and the young males who *already* make up the biking majority, and start aiming their sales campaigns at the rest of the world: the young, business-suited man with his briefcase on the luggage rack; the helmeted and suitably-clad mother giving her ditto daughter a ride to school; an older couple touring — opening up the image to bring some folks into the fold.

I read a recent road test in which the tester was complaining because one of the mirrors had "folded back against the fairing at about 105 mph." What a shame! Probably nobody'll buy the darn thing now.

Rider October 1983

European Gleanings

I've been back from Europe for several months now, yet people who haven't seen me for a while still ask, "How was your trip to Europe?" And I tell it all again — as long as they seem interested. (I think the question may be a little like asking about someone's operation.) But fragments of memories flash into my mind, lead nowhere, and are gone, kind of like a sudden flash of fireworks on a Fourth of July night.

I was wondering what going through customs in other countries would be like when, to my amazement, I didn't even make it through X-ray in NY The guard asked to check my carry-on bag. "Guess it must have been this big metal spiral on the notebook," he said, examining my MVPE (Most Valuable Piece of Equipment). I had brief visions of traveling through Europe taking all notes on my shirt cuff. If this looked fishy in NY, what would it look like in Yugoslavia? He stuck the might-have-been-bomb back in my bag and motioned me through. A writer without a notebook? About like a motorcycle without wheels.

Loner that I am, I must admit that one of the best parts of touring with a group was that I didn't have to worry about that all-inclusive and sometimes incredibly complicated business called "making arrangements." My patience under such circumstances becomes cosmic. I didn't care how long anything took; it'd all work out eventually.

On the other hand, I'm not the world's greatest traveler. Those things that I *am* responsible for loom large in my fertile imagination. Fertile? Any more fertile and I'd have a jungle in there.

Typical routine: Lie down to sleep. Pleasantly sleepy. Just about to drift into those nice gray clouds when suddenly I remember the drop of oil under my bike in the parking lot. The bed, obviously wired for electricity, short circuits and suddenly sends several thousand volts through my body. *Drop?* It was a puddle, an Olympic-sized pool. Why now? Why here? Why not in my driveway? Why not at the local McDonald's? Do they have oil in Yugoslavia? Maybe I'll have to wait till the new Siberian pipeline is finished and negotiate through three governments for a liter of oil. Maybe I'll have to stay here for months. (Maybe it *was* just a drop.)

Change of focus from anxiety to amusement: Europe doesn't seem to separate people from their dogs the way the U.S. does. You take your doggy into the restaurant with you, tie it to your chair leg, and there it waits patiently while you have your coffee and pastry. I guess that when you ask for a doggy bag there, you have living proof that you are not of a miserly nature but do indeed have the necessary qualifications to bear away these choice and expensive morsels, which of course you yourself will eat for breakfast the next morning.

I was fascinated by the prevalence of what we would call road-race leathers among not only European riders but their passengers as well. I saw a number of matching his and hers leathers and couldn't help but wonder what happens if the couple ever breaks up. Does one of them get custody of the suits so the next spouse/friend can wear one?

The only thing I wish I'd taken with me that I didn't was my soft plastic folding bucket. It flattens out to about the size of a small hand towel yet holds a bunch of water for washing the bike. I'm an obsessive bike washer on trips, finding the activity not only extremely soothing after a day on the road, but also useful in spotting problems, actual or potential. Besides, the image conveyed by a dirty bike isn't the one I want to convey, especially in a foreign country and especially with "USA" prominently displayed on my left saddlebag.

One evening as our group of six was out for a stroll after dinner, we came across six big bikes, unusually sleek and powerful for this part of the world, parked across from a sidewalk cafe. The streetlights reflected deeply enough in their lustrous paint to look like 3-D, the chrome sending up little stars, expensive helmets casually hung from handlebars or set on the seats. In the night, these bikes seemed to pulse with light like a jeweler's display of gems against black velvet. The impression was that the owners of these bikes were "high-class tough" and nobody would ever leave so much as a fingerprint on their motorcycles let alone consider stealing a helmet. We gathered around them, pointing and commenting like any other tourists, but a little selfconsciously as if the cafe had eyes and was watching us very closely. It was. The bikers, all young males, came swaggering out in their leathers and roared off into the Yugoslavian night. Cafe racers. The real thing.

As always I took many photos, but the ones I didn't take are vivid in my mind. The huge ox pulling a high-sided cart was one. I was by it too quickly, a car behind me, no good place to pull over. There'll surely be others, I thought. There weren't.

The big red stone lion carved into the side of the mountain just before our first border crossing from Yugoslavia into Italy lay indolently as if dozing in the sun, one massive paw dangling. The charm of the casual pose delighted me, but then we were around the curve and there were the border guards, passports to be checked, rain suits put away. In the busyness I forgot to ask the guards if I could go back for a minute to take that photo.

On another road a World War II airplane fighter sat alongside the road with a little park around it where tourists had gathered. Warren Goodman.(World Motorcycle Tours director) asked if I'd like to go back for a picture. For some reason I said no, realizing only later I could have learned something of interest about Yugoslavia's participation in that war that so devastated Europe.

I wonder if it's the haunting images of photos untaken that might lure me back to Yugoslavia again, or merely its glorious mountains, splendid seacoast, and friendly people who all smile in at least seven languages.

Rider November 1983

Sense Impressions

Many realizations related to motorcycling cross my mind in the form of a sentence or two and stop there, those few words seeming to comprise the life span of that thought. Nothing earthshaking, just a sense impression, a question, an observation. For example:

I don't remember ever stopping to polish a spot off my car before taking it out or ever taking my bike out *without* polishing away anything that didn't belong there.

I notice that I always turn and face into the wind as I put on my helmet, letting the wind smooth back any stray hairs that could bother me later.

If I'm on the bike and have a choice of turning left or right in a slow-speed maneuver, I'll always opt for left; it seems more natural. I have to make myself turn right from time to time just for the practice. (Where did the tradition of handling horses, and thus motorcycles, the "iron steed," from the left originate, I wonder? Seems to me it was based on a man's wearing his sword on the left (to draw with his right hand). It would interfere with his movement if he tried to mount from the right.)

Rarely do I check turn signals, headlights, brake lights, or tire pressure as I prepare to drive my car; rarely do I *not* check them all on my bike, every time.

My waving at other bikers is a matter of moods and prejudices. Sometimes I'm preoccupied and don't wave. Sometimes I'd like to wave but am busy with clutch and throttle so just nod my head. I don't wave at bikers without helmets; I can't relate to the mentality that declares, "An accident will never happen to me!"

I've never been able to street ride with the relative daring I felt in road racing: scraping toes and hanging off the seat. I simply can't assume there is no gravel in that turn, no oil slick on the freeway on-ramp. Sometimes as a result, I feel stodgy and inhibited.

How can people ride with dogs, cats, tiny children, or birds on their handlebars, gas tanks, luggage racks, and rear seats (not necessarily in that order)? I think the potential for distraction would be so great that I'd rather not ride.

Once in a campsite in Nova Scotia I rode from my tent to the river to go swimming wearing only running shoes, no socks, and a T-shirt over my bikini. I felt it was one of the more outrageous things I've done in my life.

On my bike, getting ready to pull away from a parking place, the last move I make is to pull on my gloves. It feels like a really dramatic gesture comparable to putting on my spikes at the track after I've warmed up: There now. I'm ready!

Often from a distance I try to look at my bike as if I had never seen it before. What would I think about it if it were not mine?

Would I have the nerve to race again even if someone offered me a bike, all the gear, spare parts, a trailer, and money? Motocross, probably. Road racing, I don't think so.

I always take photos on a trip. But when I *have* to take photos, everything looks different. Objects, colors, textures call attention to themselves; the whole world is more visible, more *there* than usual. I tend to ride badly then, making scenes out of the landscape ahead and to the side and watching the rearview mirror as it captures stunning shots I could take from the opposite direction.

Sitting in the sun on the first really warm day of early spring, slowly and dreamily polishing spokes, is one of the most relaxing things I can think of. But only on that one day. After that, it's a nuisance.

To ride without the set screw on my own bike's throttle seems a real chore, but on any other bike I've ever ridden, I never even think about holding the throttle on.

When people ask me these days what kind of bike to buy, I feel the same way as when I'm asked what kind of running shoes to buy. With so many models to choose from, I can't keep them all straight anymore. Whatever happened to good ol' Keds and Red Ball Jets?

The driveway at school annoys me. It always seems to have gravel at the end and across one turn so I can't ride in with a swoop and a flair.

I've always wished I could get a leave of absence so I could tour through the beautiful fall colors. (Instead, "all" I ever get is three months in the summer!)

I could do a whole book on "there oughta be a law," but one law would be that campers not be allowed to play radios any louder than just they themselves could hear.

Once in tight traffic, in separate but simultaneous reactions, I had to swerve from a car moving in on my left and my friend Dan had to stop because of a car pulling out on his right. My cylinder caught his saddlebag and cracked it slightly. I liked the way Dan described what happened: "You didn't crash into me; I stopped into you."

I like figuring out exercises to do on the bike for long hours on the road. And at nearly every stop, I run through my whole series of track warm-up stretches.

All of my longest, one-day rides – 500 miles or so — have come on the last day of a trip when I just didn't want to camp or take a motel one more time. Enough traveling! Enough $$! I just want to get home. If I were ever to try the 1000-in-1 trick, the best way would be to put me 1000 miles from home after I'd been on the road for three weeks and turn me loose. I'd take off just like a horse heading back to the barn!

Rider December 1983

Tunnel Vision

Many memories of my European trip with World Motorcycle Tours will shine always; some will eventually become dim, like the corridors and stairways in some of the energy-conscious European hotels where guests turn lights on when they enter a hallway, off when they leave. But one impression will never dim, for it was black to begin with: my worst experience, ever, on a motorcycle, and the fault was completely mine.

Where there are mountains, there will also be tunnels. And where there are tunnels, there will be darkness, for some are lighted but many are not. Rule Number One: *Do not wear sunglasses in tunnels.* Well, I always wear sunglasses during daytime riding, and not just sunglasses but dark wrap-around glasses under tinted goggles, double protection for my eyes, for I'm a contact lens wearer. A scratched cornea from road dust or debris could put a real damper on a trip, forcing me to switch over to my old prescription glasses and see everything distorted for a day or two, perhaps not able to ride.

At the first tunnel, coming on it unexpectedly, I had just plunged in, following the lights of the bike in front of me. There'd been no place to pull over to get my sunglasses out from under my goggles, no time. The sudden blackness was nearly total. I could see nothing but the red taillights of the bike ahead — no reflectors on the tunnel wall, no white line, not even my own headlight on the pavement. But the first few tunnels were short and straight, and I could orient myself by watching the lights of the bike just a few feet ahead of me and the sliver of light marking the end. I had an uneasy awareness that this procedure was definitely wrong, but it was working.

Then came the tunnel that was nearly my undoing. In I went, the light sliced off as if by a guillotine. If my bike had hurtled off a pier into an ocean of ink, the blackness could not have been denser, more overwhelming. No tiny golden opening shone at the end to tell me what direction to go in. And to my horror, the lights on the bike in front of me seemed to be changing their position in an incomprehensible way. Only afterwards did I realize that this tunnel had curved. I started to get disoriented, frightened.

Why couldn't I follow those lights? The whole tunnel seemed to start turning under and around me like a sickening amusement park ride. The inky spiral started to slip out from under my wheels just as the red lights of the lead bike disappeared completely, and I was lost.

I had no idea where I was on the road, where the road was, or the wall, up or down, left or right. Blind and dizzy, I wobbled from side to side, crossing into the other lane without knowing it, weaving back again, heading for the wall then back towards the center line again, not seeing it, not seeing anything. Terrified, sure that my trip was going to end here in the impenetrable blackness, I hung on, my throat constricted with fear, my hands in a death grip on the bars. I never even thought to do the logical thing: reach up and pull down the goggles, rip off my dark glasses. And if I had let go to do that, I probably would have toppled over, so totally disoriented had I become. My two hands on the handlebars seemed my only contact with reality.

The sudden golden half moon of daylight marking the end of the tunnel must have been as vivid a sign of salvation for me as the reappearance of the sun to a primitive tribe after a total eclipse. Weak with relief, I finally rode into the dazzling light, muttering to myself, "You jerk! You stupid jerk!"

Conrad, who'd been riding behind me, came up to me later when our group stopped to eat. "What were you *doing* back there?" he asked incredulously. "You were clear over on the wrong side of the road! You were all over the place!"

I just shook my head as he reconstructed my vertiginous careening through the darkness. "I didn't know *what* I was doing," I said, trying to explain how dizzy, how bereft of my senses I had been.

My carelessness left me badly shaken, somber for the rest of the afternoon. From then on I wore my night riding glasses with their clear non-prescription lenses under my goggles. Never mind if I did squint in the sun; at least I could see in the tunnels. Next time I'll know better. I'm grateful for the second chance.

Rider January 1984

Pride Goeth

I had just traded up from my '74 Suzuki GT250 and was now astride my dream bike, a white R60/6 BMW. Boy, was I something! I rode everywhere I could think of to show it off to everyone I even vaguely knew.

One day I took it way out into the country to show a friend of mine who used to be a biker — maybe still was; I hadn't seen him in years. But even if he and his wife were not home, it'd be a nice ride. It was and they were. And after an hour or so of basking in their admiration, I left, heading on up the dirt road I'd come down earlier. How wonderful I was, I thought as I rode along, the gravel crunching under my wheels.

The road sloped steeply up to a stop sign, one of those stop-on-a-hill-and-start-up-again situations that seem so formidable to beginners. But having so recently come up in the world, I didn't have to concern myself with beginners' problems anymore. After all, I was on a big bike now, a veteran of almost a year and 5000 miles.

The stop sign, like a flag on the peak of Mount Everest, loomed larger and larger as I approached. I felt a little flutter of anxiety as I downshifted. Gee, I wish I didn't have to stop here ... this is steep ... I can't see if anything is coming anyhow ... darn ... And I put my right foot down.

And as that foot went down and down and down, sliding on the gravel on the steep crown of the road (which I hadn't even thought of in my concern with the hill itself), my wonderfulness hit the dirt about the same time the bike and I did.

How grotesque the BMW looked resting on the right cylinder head, I thought as I awkwardly scrambled to my feet, my right knee hurting from the gravel. Because of the high crown of the road, the bike lay at a considerable downhill angle, putting it almost above me as I stood at the lowest point of the shallow ditch.

Nothing to do but pick it up, I said to myself, grabbing a handlebar and giving a tug, incredulous that this had occurred, trembling from the trauma of this disaster.

Nothing happened. The bike was apparently going to lie there forever. I tried again, suddenly covered with sweat. Nothing. I looked around the empty countryside. My friend's house was barely visible a quarter mile or so back down the road. I'll have to go back and get him to help me, I thought, and made a tentative move down the hill.

But no. Wait, I said. What if you were on a trip somewhere, alone in the wilderness? What would you do then? I'd pick it up somehow, I answered.

This time I backed up to the bike, bracing myself to use my legs, trying to keep my feet under me on the gravelly slope, cursing, grunting with the effort, sweating, feeling huge anxiety. What if I couldn't do it? Then I'd have no business being out here alone.

I heaved. The bike moved a little and started to rotate on the valve cover. The thought of the gravel scuffing that brand new bike sent a surge of adrenalin through me. A picture flashed through my mind of every muscle in my body bulging with incredible strength — a veritable Charlene Atlas! One last heave and up it came, my feet slipping precariously on the gravel slope, my body feeling awkward and unnatural against the right side of the bike. I clumsily edged it backwards down the hill to the bottom, shaking all over with the effort.

I rode the 30 miles back home, a slightly different person than I'd been when I came. Over the years it has never seemed to fail: Any time that I started to think I was pretty good, the bike would take matters into its own hands and give me a gentle reminder of at least my fallibility if not my mortality.

The calendar pages turn. The usual crowd of curious and admiring tourists had gathered to watch us "Americanskis" on our big, expensive bikes as we unloaded, this time in front of the Hotel Kanin in Bovec, Yugoslavia. And as always, murmurs from the crowd: "She's alone? Solo?" Ah yes, wonderful me again! The cosmopolitan, leather-clad world traveler.

We'd been given permission to park the four bikes up on the terrace, another of the endless courtesies shown us on our trip with World Motorcycle Tours. I only half watched tour director Warren Goodman maneuver his Silver Wing up the slick little ramp. Once up, he had to make a sharp right immediately and stop; the space was very short and narrow. It was a tricky move; I should have paid more attention.

With the others in the group busy with their own bikes, I started up, only to discover, with my front wheel up on the terrace and my rear wheel still on the ground, that the pile of luggage and the plate glass window were *right there!* Well, if He Who Hesitates is lost, She Who Hesitates tips over.

Neither foot touched anything but thin air. "Help, help, help!" Was that actually me shouting like that? All of those people standing around — surely someone would get to my side to help catch the bike; the toppling over was taking forever. But by the time my foot finally met the ground, it was too late.

As I extricated my cosmopolitan, worldly, and sophisticated self from the potted plant I had landed in, half a dozen people rushed forward to pick up the bike in six different languages. I made myself as small as possible inside the once-dashing leather suit which now felt like a costume of some sort. Who is this woman masquerading as a motorcyclist, they were no doubt wondering. My grand entrance in front of cheering thousands suddenly became a little mishap observed by a dozen tourists.

Reality. May I always remember to keep my head out of the clouds and both feet flat on the ground whenever possible.

Rider February 1984

All My Worldly Goods

Things! I guess we all feel surrounded and overwhelmed by them at times. My files at school, for example, are positively terrifying after 16 years of teaching. I could teach composition eight hours a day for the next 16 years and never repeat myself. My closets runneth over with running gear: holey warm-up pants, mismatched jackets, ancient Nikes and Adidas that have long since given up both body and sole. I found myself taking stock recently of the incomparable treasures motorcycling has added to my life since I joined the ranks of those who "Do It in the Dirt!" and anyplace else that two wheels can go.

One of my favorite and most impressive possessions is an 8' x 12' poster of the R90/S when it first came out: a breathtaking bike in 1974. This astonishing piece of art covers nearly all of one side of my garage, and given a certain light and a little ripple of wind, the bike appears to be coming, larger-than-life, right off the wall at you. The poster is held together now with tape and thumbtacks but well worth all the little repair jobs over the years. I'd wanted to put it in my bedroom originally but maybe wisely decided that

I didn't want to see a riderless motorcycle leaned at a rakish angle careening towards me every time I opened my eyes a crack.

Let's see, what else? Ah yes, my tool box. I never had my own tools till I owned a bike, and then, of course, when one went racing, one had to have a tool box. My old checklist of stuff to take to the track is still taped onto the top of the box though I haven't raced in some years. It has my name on it in crooked paste-on gold letters, and a couple of old numerals for a long-gone number plate, and a cotter pin for the axle of my long-gone 125 Suzuki — I'll keep 'em, just in case.

And of course there are the motocross boots and the chest protector and the genuine black goatskin leather pants and the dashing black long-sleeved nylon shirt with the padded elbows and "Suzuki" on the front and "Butcher" and "45" on the back. Sigh. I guess I'll keep those too. My grandson is seven months old, and if he doesn't grow too big and if he ever decides to race, well, his name is Butcher too. Come to think of it, though, I'd probably have a fit if he wanted to race. I mean, he could get *hurt* doing that!

Here's my first-ever leather jacket: a brown Brooks man's size 34 with the action pleat in the back sewed down so the shoulders wouldn't be so huge on me, and the faint outline where a big adhesive tape "X" once covered the whole back from when I road raced and had to identify myself as a beginner:

"Here rides a novice, you hot shots. Wave as you go by!"

Gloves ... if I had a dollar for every pair of gloves I've bought for riding, I'd be rich. Some work; most don't. The thumb seam is too thick and hurts my hand, or the gauntlet is too short and doesn't quite stay over my jacket cuff, or the lining is so bulky I can't move my fingers, or the glove doesn't end where my fingers do. But sometimes I get lucky. At last count I had four pair in my fairing (for hot weather, cold weather, in-between weather, and weather that hasn't been invented yet) plus six more in the closet on stand-by: worn, faded, shriveled, and torn but ready to come out of retirement for one more ride.

I'm a compulsive journal/scrapbook/album keeper anyhow. In addition to the piles of yellowing notebooks I've always used as diaries, scrapbooks on every activity from horse showing to college going, and albums on sons running, Mom running, and other family stuff, I now have piles of yellowing notebooks called "Trip Journals" (much more important sounding than "diaries"). I also keep bulging scrapbooks with photos from every race, every trip, every get together involving bikes and bikers for the last decade. Not only that, all the photo negatives are filed and labeled, all the mounted photos are dated and captioned (wittily, of course); all the albums are garishly decorated with bike stickers of every sort. Listen, when I keep records, I do it *right!*

I've got a snazzy maroon leather suit that I wear when I travel. Ordered it by mail years ago. The pants and jacket aren't quite the same color, and the jacket had to be altered so much that the side pockets now sit at an angle almost incompatible with human anatomy. For some reason, alterations were never made in the lining, though, so now there's twice as much lining as jacket. When I carry it over my arm, I make sure to keep the leather side out; otherwise I look like I'm on my way to make a bed somewhere with a pile of satin sheets. But hey — when I wear this suit, I feel important, glamorous, and *safe.* What more could anyone ask?

I have a huge pile of obsolete BMW road tests in case I decide to buy a bike that doesn't exist anymore; a bulging tech folder that will come in handy if I decide to give up teaching and become a motorcycle mechanic; first and second drafts of every *Rider* column I've done since the first one back in October of '79. (Don't famous writers donate their priceless first drafts to famous libraries for millions of dollars of tax deductions someday?); and every letter I've ever received from *Rider* readers (including one that accused me of being a feminist, told me to get lost, and speculated that I probably rode "a pink and white Honda with an automatic clutch."

But let's be sensible. I've got to get rid of some of this stuff. I guess I could throw away this left boot with the hole in the top from the shifter and the hole in the bottom to let the rain out. But the right one should still be okay. Maybe I can use it for something — it must be around here somewhere — maybe under this rainsuit with the rip down the back and the zipper that doesn't work .... Gee, I remember wearing this suit that day in Maine when I saw my first moose. I'd better keep it. What if my good one starts to leak or something?

Rider April 1984

On the Lonely Road

I had dreamed of finding such a place. The view from the campsite high on a hill in Nova Scotia was stunning. Far below, the quiet ocean lay smooth and golden in the late afternoon sun, curving into a deserted crescent beach of reddish sand After slowly, peacefully setting up camp, I'd ridden back down the road a few miles to eat in a superb restaurant that used to be a schooner, and now I was back, full of lobster, sitting alone watching the ocean turn from sunset gold to silver gray to starlit black. Tomorrow, I thought eagerly, I would ride the Cabot Trail around the tip of Nova Scotia, my glorious goal after 1,800 miles of riding. Then as I sat there, to my astonishment something very unusual happened. I felt lonely.

I don't know — maybe it was the incredible scenery and no one to share it with, although that hadn't bothered me on any of my other trips. Maybe it was because tomorrow I'd ride a loop through the Highlands National Park that would turn me around, head me towards home, and the word "home" caused a sudden contraction just a little southwest of my heart. Or maybe it was because whatever I've had to prove to myself on my other trips alone had already been proven.

And as if to prolong my somber mood, sleep seemed to have been delayed somewhere along the line. It didn't show up for the longest time, and when it did arrive, it was only half-hearted and didn't want to stay. So all night long I listened to the wind walking strangely in the grass around my tent. I don't know how many times I unzipped the tent to look around and see who was there No one.

This was not a typical experience, for usually I loved being alone on the road, in restaurants, in campsites, talking to people occasionally but for the most part feeling sort of mysteriously folded in upon myself, being quiet, writing in my journal, focusing on my moods. Usually a kind of joy pervaded my days and nights alone; being alone itself seemed to be the cause. But sometimes, in addition to loneliness, another dark dimension would intrude: fear.

Once in the hills of southern Ohio, two guys in a pickup truck played pass-me games, drinking beer and tossing the cans out along the roadside. They'd pull over up ahead, watch me go by, sit there long enough to be out of sight in my rearview mirrors. Then there they'd be again, framed in those little shivering silver circles on my handlebars, the images growing larger while my heart thumped wildly and I wondered what would happen, what to do. And then the game was over; they were gone as suddenly as they had appeared.

And the man in the yellow Mustang who followed me for miles through the mountains of eastern Kentucky, refusing to pass, slowing down when I slowed down, speeding up when I did. I'd looked at the map and thought that road would make a nice shortcut through that corner of Kentucky. Instead it corkscrewed ominously back and back upon itself, heading up and down, up and down, but never seeming to go anywhere. Nothing remotely resembled a safe place to pull off and be among people, and it was getting on towards evening. The mountain landscape seemed more and more desolate. Why had I ever taken this road? All afternoon I'd been sandwiched between coal trucks hurtling down hills behind me, creeping up the hills in front of me. In places the road had fallen away from the mountain leaving a one-lane dirt path under repair. And now this car behind me for an hour.

Suddenly I saw a little weatherbeaten store with a pleasant looking man sitting in front of it, and impulsively I whipped over and pulled in. The car went on by. I told the young man I thought I was being followed, and as I talked, the yellow Mustang came back past, slowed, and kept on going. "You just go on," the young man said kindly. "I'll keep watch, and if that guy comes back again, I'll get in my car and follow him just to be sure he doesn't bother you. But he won't catch up to you now, once you get 10 minutes ahead. You'll be OK." And an hour up the road a miraculous couple appeared, sitting on a motorcycle at an ice cream place in a little mining town They invited me home, gave me their absent daughter's bedroom and a great breakfast the next morning, instructed me to "foller this-here road ‿ till y'all get to that there road and purty soon, why you'll be somewhere afore you know it!" And I was.

And the long steel grate bridges, and the sudden violent thunderstorms with the rain sweeping sideways and the lightning crackling down all around and deep ditches and narrow berms and no place to pull over. And the half dozen rowdy, obscene drunks who pulled in, in the middle of the night, and camped next to me in a relatively deserted state park. Seeing my motorcycle parked nearby, they wouldn't know I was a woman alone, I figured, but I lay sleepless.

So I've been scared a few times on trips alone. And lonely once or twice. (And guilty of occasional understatement.) But the fear always passes and never seems so bad in the retelling. And by the same token, the joy passes too and blends into sorrow which turns again into delight, and so on. It's this constant swirl of emotion that gives a trip alone an intensity that somehow overshadows the anxiety. It's as if when I ride alone, my body is a harp that the wind plays on, touching every string, every nerve-ending. The music is frightening sometimes, but haunting. I always seem to want to hear it again.

Rider May 1984

Following Instincts

In spite of the controversy hovering over some recent exchanges of opinion on riding alone vs. riding in a group and the validity of a brother/sisterhood of motorcyclists, my own tendencies toward riding alone or with one other person are fairly well known. I drive a car but don't feel a kinship with everyone else who does, though I admit that eons ago I used to wave at VW Bugs when I drove a red '67 Beetle with huge daisy decals on its fenders — a late-blooming flower child of the '60's.

Ten years ago I waved at nearly all bikers. Then I waved at mostly touring types. Now I don't wave much at all. There are so many bikes on the road that the old image of daring, wind-in-the-face freedom seeker seems a little trite. And I typically experience a sense of mild anxiety when I'm riding alone and chance puts me alongside another rider or a group of bikes. It's based somehow on a need for privacy: certainly mine and probably theirs. I didn't invite them into my meditation; they didn't invite me to their party.

Once, I've forgotten now where — New Brunswick, I think — I got into one of those on-the-road situations where I seemed to be involved with a group of riders heading the same way at pretty much the same speed for several hours. If I pulled off for gas or food, I'd find them again on down the road as they pulled on from wherever they'd stopped. It was a group of four or five ordinary looking young men on mid-range to large street bikes with casual camping equipment tied on here and there. We'd acknowledged each other with a nod, and that was all. Seemed like no matter how fast or slowly I rode, trying to "create my own space," as psychologists are fond of saying, the traffic flow or gas stops or something kept us together.

If I stay with a strange bike or bikes on the road, I feel like an intruder. If I slow down to keep them ahead, I'm frustrated by not riding "my" speed. If I breeze on by, exceeding the speed limit to do so, I feel as if I'm showing off and also figure that the patrol car is just over the next rise. The male/female situation didn't bother me. It's just that if I'm riding alone, I'm probably out to prove something to myself about myself, and I can't use any help with that. (But boy, if you see my helmet on the shoulder, please stop. If I couldn't fix something myself, I wouldn't be feeling very independent!)

Anyhow, there seemed to be no end to the togetherness short of a change of route altogether. So what the heck. This was a pretty road; we were all members of the universal family of bikers. Just settle in and ride, I told myself. Don't be so anti-social.

The two-lane road was hilly, curvy, pretty, and smooth; the day was pleasant, the traffic sparse, the pace acceptable. The miles went by. They pulled off again, but then I needed gas later. Ah, togetherness once more.

Eventually a truck appeared behind us, sometimes close (on the downhills), sometimes far back (on the uphills). Since I was trailing the group slightly, I watched it fairly closely, but soon it became merely another part of the landscape. I didn't check my mirrors as often; the late afternoon Sargasso Sea Syndrome carried me along: becalmed in a sea of other bikes, the moving landscape, my own drowsy thoughts, I drifted through the miles "As idle as a painted ship/ Upon a painted ocean."

Then on a long downhill, whether impulsively or by previous agreement, the lead biker put on his left turn signal and rather suddenly swooped off towards a park entrance on the other side of the road. One by one the remaining bikes followed, to my great relief. Maybe that's where they were headed to camp. Maybe *this* time I'd finally be able to get back into my Greta Garbo routine again, alone at last.

However I was not quite alone. The truck had crept up on us again somewhere back there, and now on this long downhill, assuming that I was part of the group and would also be turning off, it was almost on me, apparently swinging out to pass a slower car also heading down the hill ahead of us both. I was past the park — no chance to turn in there. An oncoming car at least as big as a house filled the other lane with about the same impact on my solar plexus as the huge hurtling truck filling my rearview mirror.

This was four to five years before my first experience of lane splitting on the L.A. freeway and seven years before my initiation into riding the Alps, zipping between buses and trucks at every opportunity, real or imagined. Nothing to do but do what I'm doing, I must have decided, gluing myself to the center line and hoping for the best.

The truck WHOMPED by on my right, its wide box inches away from all that was dear to me in the world at that moment; simultaneously the oncoming car whooshed past on my left, and the car ahead of me stayed put as I followed the truck by, sucked up into a higher speed in its gigantic wake.

The silence, relatively speaking, was stunning. The sound of my own engine gradually sorted itself out from the tumultuous roar of the truck that was rapidly growing smaller on down the hill. The other bikers were gone, never to appear again. The car behind me turned to a speck in my mirrors.

The afternoon drifted back in again as if it had been away for a while. I had possession of "my own space" again though I certainly hadn't created it; that had been done for me. I was simply glad to still be in it.

The moral of this story is threefold. I learned that motorists will assume all members of a group of riders are going to do the same thing. I think I learned not to let my mirrors go blank for minutes at a time. And I hope I learned to follow the dictates of my own needs on the road. If I "vant to be alone," I'd better do something about it.

Rider June 1984

So Many Dreams to Choose From

Editor Tash Matsuoka recently asked me what bike I'd like to ride this year for our third Women's Road Test Ride. "We're calling it a Dream Tour," he said. "What would you like us to try to get for you? Give me three choices. Think about it."

After I hung up, my thoughts careened around beyond all reasonable boundaries of time and availability. If, walking down Main Street in my little town, I suddenly entered some kind of time warp and saw a store I'd never seen before (because it wasn't *there* before), and the sign said UNIVERSAL CYCLE, and underneath it said, "We Stock Every Model Ever Made," what would I choose?

I'd want to ride one of the earliest, just to see what that was like, and I'd choose a 1914 Excelsior because that's what my Uncle Earl used to ride. He died recently, so the column I did on my visit with him ("Viewing the Past," Oct., 1980) has special meaning for me now.

I'd want to ride a Vincent Black Shadow because the romance of that name about knocks my socks off. Surely one of the greatest auras in all of motorcycling hovers about that marque.

I'd want to ride a Triumph Bonneville, never mind the stereotyping about its loco British electrics and its tendency to strew nuts and bolts behind it like Hansel and Gretel's pathway of bread crumbs so they could find their way home again. All legends are entitled to a few eccentricities. I'd like to straddle its lean frame and do some leaning myself. Handling, handling! That was the name of *that* game, and I'd like to play it just once. (And how about a Norton Commando while I'm at it?)

I'd like to ride a 900 Ducati because when I used to road race there was always one in the 24 Hours of Nelson Ledges, and just remembering the intense deep sound of that bike gives me chills. My very bones seemed to vibrate with that low throbbing rumble when it went by. What would it be like to be *on* it, I wondered.

I'd like to take a really trick BMW snazzed up for roadracing the way Reg Pridmore's used to be when he was winning national production class races in '74, and slowly, slowly learn how to throw that strangely familiar machine into the turns and hurl it down the straights.

Believe it or not, I'd really like to ride lots and lots of little bikes, from 200's to 350's: the kind of bike that people really buy first to learn on, and evaluate them for "user friendliness" whether that user is a scared-to-death-but-won't-admit-it male or a scared-todeath-and-will-admit-it female. I'd like to ride a 250 Suzuki again — my first bike — to see how it feels now.

I'd like to ride some kind of Harley just once since I didn't get to ride the FXRT on our last Women's Road Test Ride, just so I can say I've ridden one. I'd especially like to ride it when I have sore muscles and could use a good massage from head to toe.

I'd like to put a ladder up to the saddle of one of the new long-legged breed of motocross bikes, obviously the result of genetic experimentation since my racing days back in '74-'75 on my stubby little TM125 Suzuki. How did they ever get that giraffe to feel sexy about a dirt bike, I wonder?

I'd like to ride a trials bike again. I've been on one only once, briefly. It was like another world. The notion of "geometry" meant something to me for the first time since 10th grade. The security and sense of control I felt as I crawled up creekbanks and slithered down hills was unreal. Now that's a kind of competition I could go for, but there's hardly any to be found in my area that I know of. I would have kept my old VW Bug just so I could practice riding over it!

Yes, I guess I'd like to ride the new BMW K100, with a combination of curiosity and resignation. Progress. I feel about it kind of the way I did when McDonald's finally came to town: a nice place to visit, and inevitable, but do I really want to eat there every day?

I'd want to ride a Moto Guzzi V50 that came out a few years back. The write up *(Rider* May, 1980) intrigued me; a couple of readers wrote to say they loved it for its handling and quickness; then it dropped out of sight — not that I'd ever seen one anyhow. But all the Guzzis seem to be rare birds, sort of like the great owls whose huge soft wings I catch an occasional glimpse of when they are suddenly disturbed by daylight. They float to another tree and disappear till darkness comes. Where are you, MG V50?

Okay, Tash, there's my list. See what you can do.

Rider July 1984

How to Ride in the Alps (or not)

With typical American big thinking in all my years of street riding, I had been accustomed to reacting if a car came within two yards of my two-wheeled space. Two yards now seemed a great vastness, an infinity of distance in which all manner of maneuvers might be accomplished. It was more like two centimeters that now provided that crucial "assured clear distance" between me and the careering Porsche, Mercedes, and BMW drivers breathing down my tail pipes; between me and the diesel-spewing bus lumbering up the two-lane mountain road in front of me; between me and the on-coming van as I whipped around the seven Yugoslavian army trucks in snake-like convoy.

Thus began my education in European-style motorcycle riding. Lane splitting once on the L.A. freeway during the morning rush hour seemed like child's play in retrospect. Here, then, are instructions for passing procedures in the Alps as they gradually became apparent to me on my first-ever European tour last summer. (Tape this list onto your windshield; you never know when you might suddenly find yourself riding through Yugoslavia.)

1. Tailgate the vehicle in front of you as closely as possible in the lowest gear you can manage without putting your feet down.

2. Shift from first gear to second and back 87 times while awaiting your big chance.

3. Peer left around the vehicle, sticking your head out through the black cloud of diesel fumes enveloping you. Do not inhale for as long as necessary.

4. Disregard configuration of center line: dotted, solid, or double — all meaningless when you are about to pass out from lack of oxygen.

5. Do not wait for clear highway ahead. (a.) There will be none, ever. Or (b.) It's no fun that way.

6. Ignore all speed limit, intersection, or tunnel signs. Variety is the spice of life. (It may also have some relationship to death, but we won't discuss that now.)

7. Notice a space about the size of a mountain goat between the truck ahead of you and the on-coming double decker tour bus.

8. Flick on your left turn signal, an act which gives you the approximate authority of God.

9. Go for it!

10. Feel your head snap back under the G forces of the acceleration you didn't know your motorcycle had. (It doesn't, but it doesn't want to die either.)

11. Turn pale as you swerve into the infinitesimal space in front of the truck you just passed and slam on your brakes to avoid embedding yourself in the trunk of the tiny Fiat six inches in front of you.

12. Look in your rear-view mirror to receive the congratulatory gesture of the truck driver, delivered in Esperanto sign language.

13. Make a mental note to look up a clinic in the U.S. that specializes in treating adrenalin addiction as soon as you get back. (Also note: Excitement is greatly enhanced if these procedures are carried out when woozy from jet lag and diesel fumes. The altered state of consciousness produced by Alpine touring may render drugs obsolete.)

14. Whenever possible, try to make all these moves in tandem with another bike. The thrill of two in a space meant for one is indescribable. And when you return home, your credentials will immediately earn you a spot on the Blue Angels precision flying team, no questions asked. After all, you have rushed in where no angel in its right mind would have trod.

15. Whenever you think your nervous system can't handle anymore, hope for rain. There's nothing like rain-slick blacktop in the steepest, curviest part of the Alps to help you relax. Now no one passes anyone. All 5600 vehicles that decided to travel the Alps on this Tuesday afternoon, including you, will slow to four miles per hour, especially after they have seen those two Grand Prix drivers in the red Porsches who were practicing for Le Mans (or were they just going for groceries? Hard to tell.) suddenly decide to perfect their spin-out techniques. The one car looks a little strange hanging out over the cliff that way while the other has made a pit stop down in that gully, but no doubt they have their reasons. In the meantime, here is a splendid opportunity to practice cornering your bike at a near standstill in a vertical position.

Ah, those were the days, my friend: life in the fast lane — when I was so worldly, so cosmopolitan, so scared!

Rider September 1984

A Hole in Time

The dust was probably the worst part.

And the mud. And waiting on the line while the race in progress screamed itself towards the checkered flag.

Six months after I started riding, I saw my first motocross race. Until 1974 I'd hardly been aware such a thing existed. Running, the first love of my life, had come nearly to a halt because of a long-term heel injury. My seemingly insatiable competitive needs were throwing out useless and dangerous sparks, like a broken high-tension wire.

A few days later a friend helped me pick out a race bike — a 125 Suzuki — and equipment. It was neat having a bike that I didn't have to worry about. If it fell over, so what? A ding in the tank, a dent in the pipe would just make it look better somehow, like a real race bike. I was pleased when my handlebar ends got scuffed, my boots dirty, my trailer scratched up. Now that stuff didn't look so new, and I didn't look so much like a beginner.

I learned how to remove, clean, and replace a chain and an air filter, and how to load and tie down the bike by myself. The simplicity of these bikes lent itself to a more casual way of handling them than I'd ever experienced with any street bike.

Before each race I walked the course with more experienced riders and marveled at how they knew what would happen as the day went on. "It'll berm up here," one would announce, looking at a flat, smooth, freshly disked turn. "You can take this one WFO," another would say seriously to me about a huge sweeper off the long back straightaway. ("Maybe *you* can," I'd think.) I can't remember how long it took me to learn exactly what "WFO" meant, but the body English and tone of voice that always accompanied it were self-explanatory.

Hitting the throttle just right to launch me off a jump....

Somehow, however incongruous it may have seemed to my old friends, this new scene felt like home. Stomping around in my multi-buckled boots, my face white where my goggles had been, the rest covered with dust, sprawling in my lawnchair or fussing with the bike between motos, I was also, not incidentally, reeling in the slack of all those years I hadn't ridden. I'd never have the courage of the fearless 14 year olds I was racing against, but I'd sure improve my riding skills.

In the winter I dug up the lawn playing in the snow with that bike (though I didn't know how badly 'til spring). Midweek in the summer I did 180s and figure eights around bushes back in the pasture. I read how-to books and went to a race riding clinic where I was not only the only female but old enough to be the mother of all the young boys there. I couldn't help but smile when one of them, not realizing there was an odd one in their midst, asked an urgent question about certain protective equipment. A great nudging of elbows and smirks in my direction wised him up into red-faced awareness. The instructor calmly answered the question with a "most of us do." Even though I didn't, we all eventually shared a good day's practice.

I found a track about 80 miles away where a dozen or more girls fiercely raced the sadly misnamed "Powder Puff' event, and most summer Sundays for a year or so were spent on that long haul. But that was what felt good at the time. And pulling into my driveway as the sun was going down, slowly unloading, tiredly putting stuff away, I felt as if I had done something important with my day. If I had a trophy to show for it, so much the better. But if I had simply ridden well and learned something, that was what really counted.

I've always kind of liked hard, hot, dirty, very physical sports, and I've loved the sound of racing engines since I was a kid going to the midget auto races with my folks back in the '40s. Things fall into place sometimes, like the pieces of colored glass in a kaleidoscope holding in a beautiful pattern before the world turns and they separate and fall with little clicks into new designs.

A beautiful pattern? The mud, the pre-race jitters, the clouds of dust into which the whole pack of bikes would disappear, the scorching sun, the deafening noise like a swarm of giant sci-fi bees gone mad — this was beautiful?

Well, yes, it seemed glorious then. Hitting the throttle just right to launch me off a jump, out-maneuvering that rider who'd been ahead of me for three laps, making a one-foot-down-pivot-the-bike-throw-up-a-rooster-tail turn — these seemed beautiful. Even the long drive home in my yellow VW Bug crammed full of gear, the little two-rail trailer bouncing and clattering along behind carrying the beat-up yellow bike, felt like a fine end to a fine day.

Things seemed simpler back then, the way they always do. During a race I was too busy keeping the bike under control to be scared. "Whoa!" I'd say out loud when I'd nearly go down. "Uhhnngh!" I'd grunt as I'd careen through gut-wrenching ruts. I loved it. Now, 10 years later, I approach a detour sign with a sudden sense of shock. "Gee, I hope it's not deep gravel. Gosh, I hope it's not too rutty. Boy, I hope I don't slide in this mud!" Whatever happened to good ole #45 with the toughest name at the track, "BUTCHER," in big white letters across the back?

The kaleidoscope has turned. The falling pieces click with a sound like a clock ticking. Somehow a little hole in time opened for a while back then and let me make up for something I'd never had a chance to do as a kid. It was wild and crazy, and I hurt my knee once and limped proudly for a week afterwards.

Maybe it was all just dirty and noisy and dangerous. But now the scene is bathed in the golden light of an early summer's evening in my memory as I make that long drive home from the track, the yellow bike bobbing in my rearview mirror. I sure had a good time.

Rider October 1984

The Other Road

"Did you make any exotic motorcycle trips this summer?" someone asked me recently. I had to think for a minute. Flying out to California to ride for a week last May didn't seem to count — not that California isn't exotic (it certainly is to my Midwestern eyes), but I didn't think that was what he meant. To me a motorcycle trip should start from my own garage on my own bike. So I responded, "How about Buffalo? Does that count?"

He smiled and wandered away. I guess in his mind, it didn't. But for me it seemed to have been an oasis at the end of a hectic summer. The obvious way to go from Cleveland to Buffalo is on the freeway. The less obvious way is to meander along Lake Erie the old way, Route 5.

The old way. Every area has a road called "Old Route Something or Other." It's what used to be the main road until the freeway or the thruway or the turnpike or the toll road was built.

Sometimes you catch glimpses of it as it parallels the new road where you're zooming along. Sometimes it's been abandoned: a fading white concrete path, its edges blurred with weeds, its joints breaking apart and turning green under the inevitable encroachment of the grass. More often than not, though, it's still in use and may take you on a direct route into the past.

Along this road are the small towns with their beautiful old homes where people are actually sitting on their porches in the evening or on a Sunday afternoon. There'll be an old inn that used to be a stagecoach stop where you'll have one of the best meals you've ever eaten, served family style with bowls heaped with food on the table so you can help yourself. You'll never be able to find this inn again; it disappears as soon as you leave, as does the town. "I'd swear we came down this road, and it was just around that bend...."

In the countryside the cows are heading single file for the pasture in the early morning, and the kids in the schoolyard in front of the tiny school that hasn't been consolidated and boarded up yet wave as you ride by.

The old man at the old two-pump station with the funny looking pumps takes you inside to show you a picture of himself on his old Indian and tell you what riding was like before even Old Route Something or Other was there, when it was just a gravel road. "I'll never fergit that time I was ridin' by the light of the moon 'cause my headlight didn't work and I hit that cow doin' about 50 — I was doin' the 50, the cow weren't doin' nothin', 'specially after I hit 'er, but by then neither was I...."

The thruway moves away from the lake as if to say that anything pleasant to look at is outside the definition of such a road, But the old road knows what's best for you, and takes you there and keeps you there for as long as you want to be unhurried and at peace with yourself.

Lake Erie is the most dangerous of the Great Lakes, I'm told: so shallow that stormy winds whip it into a frenzy in moments. But today a collage of sailboats appears through a frame of trees: a dozen disembodied white wings pasted onto a polished cobalt-blue canvas. I feel a sense of kinship: the white sails against the water, my white bike against the sky. White is for good guys, for purity, for innocence: may I always have a sense of wonder at each new mile down the road, and for each place I've never seen before.

Western New York is dotted with wineries, and the vineyards stretch toward the horizon, pulling your eye down their dark parallel rows in a dizzying pattern as you ride by. Fruit and vegetable stands appear like sudden bright multicolored flowers every few miles. The array of produce is dazzling. I want to stop and buy one of everything, but my saddlebags are already pretty full.

Somehow the Old Route always has a little motel that appears at dusk with another bike parked in front of it and rooms for $12 a night and a claw-footed bathtub instead of a shower and a Ma and Pa behind the counter who show you photos of their grandchildren and call you by your first name even before you sign in. (This motel will also disappear, just like the old inn did.)

I did take an exotic trip this summer. On my way to Buffalo I didn't know what time it was, or what year, and I didn't care. The

200 miles were a kind of Twilight Zone, a boundless, timeless road from Here to Wherever. I hope the road, too, will not have disappeared the next time I need to ride it.

February 1985

The Secret Life

In *The Secret Life of Walter Mitty* by James Thurber, the main character daydreams his way into greatness, and although I've had my share of adventures, still I can fantasize about many more I may never have. I can also fantasize being a completely different kind of person from what I am.

I wake up one morning in the summer after a solid eight hours sleep, wander downstairs, leisurely prepare a large breakfast, which I eat while I peruse the morning paper. About the time I finish the funnies, I remember that — oh yes, this is the day I am leaving on my 20,000-mile solo trip to wherever my bike decides to take me.

Within half an hour all loose ends are tied up in the house, yard, and community; I casually don my leathers with nary a butterfly to be felt, and swoop out of the driveway and onto the road in a beautiful arc for the camera crew that is making how-to films for beginning riders.

Distaining all freeways, I head off into the, well, more-or-less sunrise, humming a haunting fragment from my new Zamfir album. A mile up the road, I skillfully thread my way through the pack of wild dogs that has been terrorizing the county (rendering the leader kaput with a booted toe to the skull), avoid the drunk driver careening over the top of a blind hill directly at me (a mere flick of the wrist is all it takes), and decide just for fun to slalom at 80 mph through the orange cones marking the construction site I'm passing through (I never ride more than 80 mph while cornering on gravel).

Well out into the country, I crank it up to 120 for a few hours and settle back to enjoy the ride. Umm, the bike is so smooth, and not even at redline, but why press my luck.

In the next state, before it even dawns on the Highway Patrol what that white blur was, I slow down and pull into an elegant restaurant for lunch, Before I have the sidestand down, the owner (who has a sign out saying *Motorcyclists Welcome)* has the red carpet rolled out across the parking lot, and when I take off my helmet and he sees that I am none other than the famous Grace Butcher, he is beside himself with joy. Of course I will sign an autograph for his little nephew who just loves my column.

After my free lunch, my free bike wash, my free week's supply of candy bars, my free lifetime pass to the restaurant, and my free massage, I mount up, give the assembled staff a gracious salute, and motor elegantly on out as they cheer wildly, incredibly grateful that I have appeared to add a touch of excitement to otherwise humdrum lives.

Several states, several days later, I pass a road-race track and can't help but pull in. Famous ex-racer that I am, of course I am invited to ride the next practice session. Turning down all offers of 1100 Kaws, the 900 Ducatis, the 750 Suzys, I ride my full-dress BMW (pack still securely bungeed on behind) onto the track, and after a lap or two to feel things out, crouch even tighter down over the tank and blow everybody's doors off (well, side panels anyhow). I am scraping everything — pegs, knees, valve covers — the crowd is going wild, and it's a new track record, of course.

"No, no thanks," I say to all offers to ride that day's sprints. "I don't race any more, ya know — just tour. Thanks anyhow." And to a standing ovation from the crowd, the pit crews, and all the racers, I take an easy lap, waving and smiling, ride out the gate and down the road, feeling no qualms about leaving it all behind.

That night, having ridden late, I easily maneuver my bike into the most secluded and inaccessible campsite on the pitch-black mountainside, have a fire going in minutes in spite of the wet wood from torrential rains the day before, and prepare my filet-mignon — with mushroom sauce — and Baked Alaska for dessert.

My tent does not leak or fall down in the monsoon that night, and the next morning with a skill that defies description I slide and skitter the big white bike down the muddy ruts on the washed-out trail, whistling the exciting part of the William Tell Overture ("Hi Ho, Silver! Away!") Where the path is completely gone, I simply drop down the three-foot, shale-covered bank and ride calmly downstream along the bottom of the raging creek, negotiating slimy boulders and small waterfalls like any good trials rider. Perfect ride, of course — never put a foot down once.

Settling in for a wet day's ride (I never ride more than 100 mph on unfamiliar mountain roads in the rain), I sing snatches of "Stormy Weather" as I whip through the S-curves and switchbacks on roads just barely clinging to the mountainside (no guard rails, of course). Which mountains? Gee, I really don't know — Rockies, Appalachians? I guess I just wasn't paying any attention to whether I went east or west. Doesn't matter — I've got all summer.

Stopping in briefly at the national rally to present the advanced tech seminar, I greet old friends, solve a number of bizarre never-seen-before mechanical problems for the BMW factory crew, direct the packing and shipping home of the new top-of-the-line bike that I have just won in the drawing, and leave to a standing ovation from the 2,768,964 rally goers.

A few miles up the road I can't resist stopping at a local motocross race where I win the open division handily even though my pack does fly off when I land after the biggest jump. Crazed fans fight for the privilege of returning it to me, and I leave in a cloud of dust to a standing ovation ....

Well, there's a book called *Zen and the Art of Archery* in which the would-be archers practice every move mentally for months, years before they ever touch a bow. Then *zing!* Bullseye! So all right, already. I'm practicing — just practicing!

Rider August 1982

Illustration by Robert Heindel

So Much Depends upon a Red Tent

From ***Sports Illustrated*** February 3, 1975

The best part? There were a lot of best parts. Depends on my mood when I look back on the trip.

But the *very* best part was being alone. I don't quite understand that about myself — this lifelong love of being alone. I suppose being an only child is a big part of it. I just grew up doing things alone. Feels natural now, as if that's how it's supposed to be. And besides, I get along with myself better than with anybody else I know.

Joyously riding alone, never having to ask someone, "Shall we stop here? Do you want to turn off up there? Are you ready to go now? Should we camp here?" — that was the best part of all.

And the riding! That's all I had to do, day after glorious day, my white BMW *R60/6* under me humming quietly through the blue and green and golden world. The bike was new. I'd had it only long enough to put 1,200 miles on it and have it checked over before I took off. It was my second bike (my third, really, if you count the 125 Suzuki Challenger that I'd started racing several months before). But my second street bike.

I'd had my first lesson on a full-dress BMW R75/5 and had fallen in love with it. "When I get good enough," I said, "I'm going to have a BMW." In about a year, I figured. And I rode my little Suzuki GT 250 thousands of miles through the northeastern Ohio winter while people kept asking, "Gee, isn't it a little cold to be out on that thing?" I had to ride. I had to get good enough.

Gradually I got better. I had to get better than I was that first day in the last week of October '73. That was when I went out to the garage alone the first time to start up my first bike and ride it after an hour or so of lessons the day before in first and second gear, stopping, starting, and turning, (or rather, lurching, stalling, and wobbling).

After 20 minutes of fumbling with switches, frantic and clumsy kicking, a call to the dealer to find out why it stalled every time I tried to put it in first gear ("Rev it up a bit," his wife said. "It's new; everything's tight"), drenched with sweat I got the bike out of the garage. Only stalled it three or four times (between the garage and the end of the driveway, that is). From there I managed to avoid going in the ditch on the far side of the road as I swung out with what I hoped would be flair and what ended up as a gigantic, lopsided wobble. I made a mental note to write the highway commissioner about widening the county roads. My self-image was in jeopardy.

But I rode over a hundred miles that day. And the next day. And the next. A week later, shivering violently in pouring rain and 45° temperatures, I took my riding test, passed, and sang at the top of my voice all the 15 miles back home.

Carefully, intensely, I piled up the mileage. Carefully one day I rode far out into the country and on a deserted road red-lined it through the gears to learn what the bike could do. Carefully I puttered through shopping centers, got groceries, did errands, rode to class. Carefully I rode fast on the freeways and slowly in traffic, with interest over rain grooves and with fear over the open steel grillwork of bridges. I rode thousands of miles alone and once in a while with a friend. Carefully that following summer I learned to race motocross and won a couple of trophies in powder-puff events. Gradually I was starting to feel good enough.

And then one day I walked into the cycle shop and there stood a brand-new white BMW. I'd never seen a white one. And I said to myself (and to anyone else who would listen), "O.K., Grace. I think you're ready for a BMW."

Two weeks later I took off on a 2,500-mile camping trip through New England and Canada. And the best thing of all was being alone with my bike the whole time. It just seemed as if that was how it was supposed to be.

I put up a red nylon tent in the orchard and practiced sleeping in it...

I had camped once, but I'd just stood and watched while a friend put up the tent, made the fire, cooked the meal, and packed up afterward. So before I left, I put up a red nylon tent in the orchard and practiced sleeping in it so it would seem like home on the road. Oh, I was far from the house — at least 50 yards. The rustlings in the bushes at night! Apples thunderously falling to the ground in the dark! Leaves crashing onto the tent and sliding and scratching down the sides! Good thing I practiced. Zipping myself into the tent and then into the sleeping bag produced claustrophobia of alarming proportions.

But within a few days I was sleeping well. Once, when I was told it had rained the night before, I was incredulous. Hadn't heard a thing. And so, another best part of the trip was going to sleep once all the camp chores were done, feeling the earth under me. I used no mattress, just let my body melt down around any unevenness of ground under the tent. I'm Capricorn, an earth sign. If that means anything, maybe that's why sleeping on the ground felt so good. I felt as if the whole planet was under me, holding me. A secure feeling. And outside, the bike would be parked and chained as close to the tent as I could get it. It looked massive and comforting, white in the moonlight, wet with dew, chrome gleaming quietly.

Everything I needed was in one compact roll and two small saddlebags loaded up the night before I left. That morning when I came bounding out of the house in new leathers, feeling rather self-conscious, I got down to reality quickly enough when my first tug didn't even budge the loaded bike off its center stand. "Oh Lord," I said out loud, with a weak grin in case *Candid Camera* was watching.

But the second or third tug got the bike down, and I was ready to leave. Even as I coasted backward down the slight slope of the driveway into the turnaround spot, though, I realized that this bike, which was still unfamiliar and a hundred pounds heavier than my other one, would handle differently with the load it now carried.

As I rode through the town of Chardon on my way to the freeway I began to feel like a worldly biker — full leathers, a big bike, and all my worldly goods (more or less) tied on behind. And when I reached Route 90 and swooped (yes, with flair even!) down the ramp, checking out traffic, sun and blue sky in one glance, I said (out loud to myself, of course), "Well, here I go!" Not an especially original line, but the situation was original enough to make up for it. I, who had never even put up a tent in all my 40 years till two weeks before — I, who had never gone on a long motorcycle trip — I, who hadn't even been riding a year — I was leaving on a 2,500-mile camping trip on my incredibly fine bike, alone. I sang Moody Blues' songs and was amazingly happy.

Like fragmented, colored pieces in a kaleidoscope, images of each day's ride turned, changed, fell through my mind as I sat those nights writing in my journal by the light of a candle lantern. I loved that piece of equipment. A candle burns with a most peaceful flame.

All the trip long, people in cars waved and smiled. Mostly kids and, strangely enough, old ladies. I wondered about that and finally decided that the gray-haired gadabouts had reached a point in their lives when they realized most strongly that what life is *for,* if it is for anything, is to find out what you do well, and then *do* it, for heaven's sake, before it's too late. One group of ladies passed me, giving me a real lift with their big smiles and their waves. And coincidentally, we happened to stop at the same restaurant farther down the road. As I was taking off my gloves and helmet and brushing out my wind-tangled hair, one came bustling over to where I still sat on the bike. "I just wanted to tell you that we think you're just the bravest thing!" she beamed. "I said to the girls, 'My, just think how the wind must be blowing in her face!' And here you are out here all by yourself. We think that's just wonderful!"

I smiled, modestly accepting the Wonder Woman image, and made a long acceptance speech extolling the joys of being female and being alone, riding a motorcycle. I found myself giving the same speech many times during the following weeks, and I never tired of it.

And so it went. I'd wondered, frankly, if I'd get hassled along the way. But people were only friendly, curious, helpful, courteous, interested. The bike was such a conversation piece that I'd get into discussions at traffic lights about the virtues of a shaft-driven engine (very virtuous!); at stop signs about what those things were sticking out on the sides ("Those are the cylinders, sir"); about how ghostly quiet the bike was ("Hey, is that thing running?"), and why couldn't *all* motorcycles be that quiet.

Mostly I'd ride along not too fast, just murmuring "Oh!" and "Gee!" as I'd top another hill and be wonderstruck by the next panoramic view. Is there any more striking combination of trees than clusters of white birch, stark and chalky against dense pine forests? One day, camping by a mountain lake in Maine, I found several pieces of birch bark and wrote letters. I'd always wanted to write a letter on a piece of birch bark. I felt like the Indian I used to pretend I was when I was seven.

Beauty everywhere. Even asbestos mines in Quebec were amazingly beautiful. They looked almost like natural gray canyons, and the piled-up asbestos like white mountains. Posing themselves against the backdrop of one of these "mountains" were four boxcars — two brown, one red and one green — and before them a sweep of green and golden meadow. I just sat and looked. The beauty of the mining area was astonishing.

Sometimes I'd feel so full of the scenery that I'd stop looking at it for a while and just get into the rhythm of the road. Hills and curves, curves, curves. No, I wasn't scraping the foot pegs or the valve covers. But even now I remember the rhythm of those curves as I'd climb and plunge and letter-S through mile after mile, enclosed on both sides by deep pine forests of unforgettable scent.

Truly, I felt as if I had ridden into the pages of every motorcycle magazine I'd ever read. I could see myself — wine-red leathers, immaculate white bike, blue pack — against the pines, the startling silver-blue of lakes, red and brown and gray rock walls, the curves of flower-strewn meadows — moving through all the colors and textures.

What would I *do* with this trip, I wondered. How would I use it? What would it eventually mean to me? I pondered sometimes as I rode, or as I sat writing by candlelight, or as I washed my face with dew in the early mornings. How would I be different after I got home?

"But weren't you afraid?" People always asked that later.

No. Except once. Once in Quebec the road went off in two different directions. My way, or so I thought, went across a bridge. And the bridge was that biker's nightmare: an open metal grillwork, slippery as ice, that sends the front wheel of a bike off in every direction. There's nothing to do but do nothing — to sit there, muscles frozen into an attitude of relaxation, hands holding the handlebars with a gentleness born of terror, for you must let the bike find its own way across.

Finally on the other side, I began to glory once more in the countryside, the road curving along a river lined with birches. But I started to notice that either the sun was going in the wrong direction or I was. After about 10 miles I stopped and checked my map. I had to go back over that damn bridge.

Quebec. How could I have forgotten that it is French-speaking? As I crossed the border I felt a combination of dismay, amusement, and eagerness. I'd always thought I was pretty good in high school and college French. Now we'd see.

It was O.K. Vocabulary came rushing back. At one point, after I'd set up camp and walked away for a bit, I returned to find half a dozen adults around my bike. And I could talk to them with eagerness and enthusiasm (though probably sounding like a 6-year-old) about the mechanical wonders of the bike. *"Il n'y a pas de chaine,"* I could say, gesturing-at the chainless rear wheel and pointing out the enclosed drive shaft. I could answer questions about mileage, comfort, my route, my own brave self. *"Seule? Vous etes seule? Vous etes si brave!"* I liked to hear it in any language.

Once I chose a cabin instead of my tent. It was tiny, on the shore of the mighty St. Lawrence, 20 miles wide at that point and masquerading as the ocean, with tides and sea gulls and a fine driftwood tree washed up on the beach to lean against. I built a fireplace of stones, cooked, ate, then sat with a cup of my special mix of hot chocolate and coffee, watching the sun set and the tide come in.

I had been sitting in the dark, on the red-brown sand, my pack against the water-washed smoothness of the tree trunk. But gradually I slumped farther and farther down till just my head was against the tree and my body relaxed in the sand. My fire was only embers, an orange crescent of moon had brightened with the approach of darkness, the tide had come to within a few yards of my feet. I lay there for a long time, scarcely moving. I could not have been more content.

There were times when I could escape my own observation. So often, perhaps because of my obsession with writing, I found myself mentally recording something I was in the process of doing as if I'd already done it, picturing myself telling someone about it in the future. It was hard sometimes not to feel as if I were constantly posing for some invisible photographer. It was hard to get away from *watching* myself at some beautiful spot, and simply *be* there.

But here, or on the night shore of a mountain lake listening to the loons, or wrapped in the sensuous golden day that seemed to pour itself down over the Vermont hills as I curved and flowed along the black and gray roads — here, on this trip was a kind of spontaneity that I'd never experienced. And my contentment had no particular structure other than knowing that I'd camp somewhere late in the afternoon and leave again sometime in the morning. No structure. No telephone ringing. No papers to grade. Nothing to do but tend to my bike and to myself. Nothing to do day after shining blue day but ride. Except for a few calls home to my teen-age son, no one knew where I was. And for once, I didn't care that no one knew where to find me or when I'd be back.

I'd look down at the great silver sunbursts of my cylinders, feel the power waiting quietly under my right hand. Everything I could possibly need was in my blue pack, my black saddlebags. I could feel the sun through my leathers, smell the scent of pine for days.

My old aunt and uncle in their farmhouse on 150 acres in the Adirondacks. Hadn't seen them for years. Eighty-five years old he is, and his big-game-hunting license was on the dresser in the room where I slept. My aunt cooked for me and reminisced about my parents and made me feel loved. I rode away feeling I'd found part of my family again.

"Hi! Nice bike," said the guy at the stoplight somewhere in New Hampshire. "You should take those metal covers off your plugs because they'll short out in a rainstorm. Mine did when I took a trip back in '72."

"What part of Ohio you from? I'm from Cincinnati," said the boy wearing the cross-country T shirt in the restaurant parking lot somewhere in western New York. So we talked about cross-country running and cross-country riding and how neat they both were.

"By cracky," said the white-haired, pleasant gentleman in the tiny post office in Somewhere, Maine (people *do* say "by cracky" in New England), "I got me this son of a gun of a crick in my back yesterday morning — don't your back bother you on that machine?"

The people. That was another best part. One old couple outside an old inn, standing, looking at my bike. I spoke to them as I was leaving, and they offered to tear some pages out of their where-to-camp book for me. ("I have my own, thanks, but I sure do appreciate .... ")

And the gas-station attendant in Quebec who answered my questions about the white "mountains" and sent his son inside to get me a piece of asbestos — shiny black rock with what looks like cotton fibers sticking out of it — so I could show it to my friends back home.

And the two little boys, whose grandparents ran the campgrounds, showing me the best, prettiest, most isolated spot by a stream to pitch my tent, and who ran along with me a mile or so as I jogged for a while that evening.

And the three adults who'd seen my bike in a restaurant parking lot and came in, looking for someone with a helmet who must belong to the bike so they could ask questions about how I liked it. "It's not your *husband's?* It's not your *boyfriend's?* It's *yours?"*

How nicely tired I was each night after eight hours or so on the road. How early I went to bed, and how early I woke and with what eagerness! Moving carefully inside my red tent in the morning, drops of condensation clinging like rubies to the sides, gleaming in the morn-ing light. Fold up the tent wet — it'd dry in my pack from the heat of the sun on that day's ride. I was glad the tent was red. Every morning started with a glow.

I washed and polished the bike when it needed it or when I felt the urge. Very soothing to rub and polish the long dazzling pipes, the plain clean lines of the tank and fenders. Changed plugs once. Changed the oil once. Had the steeringhead bearings tightened once. Put air in the tires once or twice. The bike gave a lot and asked little.

I always had some what-ifs on my mind. What if the bike breaks down? New bikes don't break down. What if there are no gas stations? There are *always* gas stations. What if a runaway logging-truck comes careening around a curve on the wrong side of the road up there in the middle of nowhere?

My long hair is always in pigtails when I ride, and sometimes they blow in my face because my windshield changes the airflow. I like motorists to know I am female, so I don't tuck my hair under my helmet. And as a result, I've never yet experienced any of the hostility that male bikers so often report. But one day I thought, "The heck with it. I'll just tie my hair back. It'll be out of the way." And shortly after that I stopped at a gas station to ask directions. Walked in without taking off my helmet or goggles. And the station attendant said pleasantly enough, "Yes, sir, what can I do for you?" Back came the pigtails and my identity.

Some guy on a very noisy bike appeared alongside once and nodded and smiled as if he thought he'd found a traveling companion. I was annoyed. The noise of his engine compared to mine soon gave me a headache. And the last thing I wanted on my trip was company. Doing it alone was the whole point. Finally we rode in under the golden arches of that famous and ubiquitous restaurant, our first chance to talk since he'd joined me. "Hope you don't mind my boogieing along with you," he said. "Well," I answered, "as a matter of fact. ... " And I just told him in a friendly way how it was with me. "Oh, O.K. That's cool," he said and went boogieing on his way. No problem.

As one man put it someplace where I stopped for gas, "To see a woman like you on a bike like that ... well, you have all my respect. I can't imagine any guy would ever hassle you." And none ever did. I'm 5' 6", 115 pounds. It wasn't my size that kept anyone from bothering me. It was something else. It was just what I was doing, I guess.

Busy. I sometimes felt very busy on my trip, once I'd stopped for the day. Unloading the bike, setting up camp, making a fire if I chose to, cooking, eating, cleaning up, arranging stuff in the tent, writing after all was taken care of — there seemed to be a great deal to do, and darkness seemed to come quickly. I was seldom awake after 10 p.m., seldom slept past five or six.

Making a fire that would burn right gave me great pleasure. I had to scrounge wood, and then stones with which to confine it. I had to be patient and not try to cook over the first high flames.

Once, I cooked a mixture of hamburger, hot dog, olives, cucumbers, egg, and a can of pea soup because that's what I had. It was delicious.

Once, by a river I found a thin flat stone to turn the fried eggs since I had no spatula. And I scoured the utensils with sand and dirt. It all made sense.

One thing I did not care for was threatening weather, riding with frequent glances up and around, checking the ominous clouds, always wondering if I should stop or keep going. But the weather was, on the whole, quite fine. I was rained in only one day, and that happened to be the time along the St. Lawrence that I had chosen the cabin instead of my tent.

I was quite happy at being rained in. The previous day's ride had covered only about 100 miles, all against a huge, hot wind, and I was glad for a cool rainy day. I'd ridden in a little rain to the nearby town and brought back enough food for six people. I lay on the bed, which nearly filled the one-room cabin, gazed out at the great river, whose endless sound filled my head, quieting me.

Gray sky, gray water,
Creating no horizon.
Where does the world end?

I remembered a haiku I'd written years back. Sensuously, I ate, dozed, ate, wrote postcards, dozed, ate, wrote, and finally slept. Everyone needs such days.

Sometimes I was disappointed to see what tourists call "camping." Camping at some sites I saw would have been like living in apartments, only outside. Numbered cubbyholes with bushes instead of walls. TV. Radio. Women walking around in bathrobes with their hair in rollers. Electric razors. I didn't stop at those places.

One beautiful warm, clear morning I just got up, put on shorts and a T shirt and walked into the surprisingly warm water of a mountain lake in Quebec. It was just sunrise; no one was around. Briefly the thought entered my mind, "Should I go swimming here alone?" I answered myself, "Yes, do it. For once, be different. Forget about the shoulds and shouldn'ts for a while." I felt exhilarated and peaceful at the same time. I wish there were more lakes at sunrise in life.

Gray sky, gray water...

When I came back across the border, feeling tense and excited at the crossing as if I were a spy, the friendly customs man talked bikes to me a bit as if to disarm me, then sprang *the* question: "What did you bring back with you that you didn't have when you came over?" I thought hard, desperately wanting to be honest. "Uh, two apples, two peaches, a can of chicken, and a piece of asbestos." (Oh, Lord, I was transporting *minerals* across the border!) He laughed. "Well, you didn't do much for the Canadian economy," he said and motioned me on.

Wow! I was back in the States! I could speak English again. Vermont, I love you. I was surprised at how good that simple crossing felt. The lush small farms fit just right in the valleys of Vermont. It looked different immediately. It was the United States.

It was a fine thing, all told, to be riding all day, every day, to be alone and silent, to lay a decent fire and cook a simple meal, to sit with my back against a white birch looking out over water with a cup of coffee in my hand as the sun went down, to be gently tired from the road and comfortable on the ground under a red roof.

The big white bike was always patiently nearby, forgiving of some of my early clumsiness, always starting at a touch, quietly humming over the hills and puttering through the towns, making friends wherever we went. I would look at it last thing at night before closing my tent and first thing in the morning. This trip was only the beginning. As William Carlos Williams might have put it,

> *So much depends*
> *upon*
> *a red tent*
> *glazed with dew*
> *beside the white*
> *motorcycle.*

Q: Why do you want to race?
A: Because my name comes apart

From ***Whatever It Takes***
Farrar, Sraus and Giroux, 1999

Loading up the motorcycle. Tugging on the tie-downs to secure it on the trailer. Heading through the countryside, through a little town: Main Street with the teenagers hanging around the pizza place staring at my bike, the racy little white Yamaha RD250. I am proud to be the driver of this car with the bike on the trailer behind it. People don't expect to see a girl driving the car.

A girl. Am I not supposed to say that about myself now that I am forty-four? My body is a girl's. My long hair is a girl's. From a distance people think I am a girl. From inside I think I am a girl. In bed with my lover I am a woman, but here, now, driving this car to the racetrack, I am a girl.

When I was indeed a girl, I pretended to be an auto racer. My balloon-tired Schwinn was my race car, my Indy car, my blue No. 5 Offenhauser. I lied intensely to my little friends about being a real auto racer at night when they were in bed. For some reason my mother aided and abetted me in this lie; she *almost* verified it, never scolded me, allowed my friends to believe me by not telling them anything different. Now I think maybe my mother *wanted* me to be a race car driver. Or wished she were one herself. People used to gasp when she drove our family car *50* m.p.h.! She loved it. You see? My mother was skinny and loved to drive fast. She was always a girl.

...tthe racy little white Yamaha RD 250.

My motorcycle is not a race car, but it is what has come into my life now. It is almost the same thing except that I ride it like a horse. It can go so incredibly fast with a flick of my wrist that it could leap out from under me. I lean over it, wrap my legs around it. I am perhaps in love.

I pull in through the gates at Nelson Ledges, the road-race track. "Hi, Grace!" Ah, they know me here, seem glad to see me.

I park the car, make myself stroll casually into the big barn for registration. I want to run, to leap around saying, "I'm here! I'm here!" I happily sign all the papers that deal with death and damage and destruction and disaster and doom. (Whose? Not mine, surely.)

And being with my bike-race friends in the shadowy tents and vans of the darkening infield, sitting by the bike-race campfire in my bike-race chair, toasting my bike-race hot dog ... yes, I am here among these people to do this amazing thing, to ride the 100 m.p.h. I am afraid to ride on the street where cars and dogs and loose gravel and chuckholes all leap out to bring me down. Here there is a clear clean track for me to go fast on, and corner workers who speak to me with silent sudden flags of many colors that tell of oil spills and accidents ahead and one lap to go — corner workers who will run to me if I should fall. Here there is an ambulance, quietly, quickly coming just for me should my body explode onto the pavement in that terrible surprise of knowing I have crashed.

And tech — the late-night laughter in the brightly lit building where we've pushed the bikes through the ruts and dark and dust of the infield. The bikes go through tech inspection. They are declared safe, for look here — here is proof: This is safety wire so nothing falls off the bike except the rider. My skintight leather road-race suit is looked at. It is declared safe, for here is all the padding that rounds the angles of my skinny body and here are all the zippers that zip me into this additional layer of brown leather skin that has my name on the chest in white letters. And my helmet that may bounce on the pavement so my head does not. Ah yes, I am safe as long as I do not fly over the crash wall and drown in the swamp or cross paths with the woodchuck who ambles across Turn One at least once on every race day.

Push the bike back through the dark voices of my friends, through the dark summer night with its red jewels of campfires, through the dark butterflies that rise from somewhere with wings so gentle they seem almost not to be made of fear but of summer wind, through the dark rows of trucks and vans and families and babies and dogs and children. This would be like a picnic tomorrow if it were not for what some of us are going to do.

I pretend to sleep and morning pretends it is never going to come. But finally we stop pretending and I do and it does. Riders' meeting. I am a rider. I am amazed by this, every time. I am again going to do this unreal thing that only incredibly brave young men seem to do. Am I therefore brave by association? I am the only girl in this boisterous gathering. I listen intently as the race director explains the upcoming practice session to us. I look serious or keep my face carefully neutral but laugh at the jokes.

Instructed in the protocol of practice, we leave the hot, crowded little room in the stands. The track shimmers and curls off into the distance like a thick gray snake in the sun. At my campsite in the infield I struggle and wiggle into my leathers on this sticky hot Ohio morning — like a snake myself now, writhing around to get back into my skin. Now my loins are girded, my feet are booted, my hands gloved, my head helmeted, my pigtails tucked in. *Now.*

Kicking my bike into action I ride slowly through the pits to line up for practice. Where are my friends who also ride this class, the 250 Production class? I keep looking for the big X taped on the backs of the leather jackets of the beginners, the first-year racers. My own X in silvery duct tape from shoulders to waist seems to burn into my back: a reminder. Veteran riders will watch out for me, be aware that I might do something squirrely out there, something they wouldn't do. While I am waiting, I pray. I also pray while I'm riding: "Please, dear God ... " (hurling the bike around the 80 m.p.h. first turn), "Keep me safe ... " (scraping my toe in the fast left-hander), "Let the light be around me ... "

(speedometer needle touching 100 m.p.h. on the back straightaway).

Practice session. Another one. And the first race. As I line up on the track with twenty other bikes, all of us revving it up — that shrill, sharp, racketing two-stroke howl drowning the pounding of my pulse, drowning all my thoughts — I am turning my throttle, turning it ... turning it ... till the green flag swoops suddenly down and I am doing this wild and crazy incredible thing. Going as fast as I dare, feeling good true lines through the turns, hauling my bike down nearly on its side to keep my line, to stay on the track. Getting passed, being whooshed by better riders as they go by. Amazed that I'm going as fast as I can and they are passing me. No, I'm not going as fast as I can, only as fast as I dare.

Spot a friend ahead of me, concentrate on moving up lap by lap, maneuvering, passing him at last when he goes a little wide on one turn. At last! Ah! A small ecstasy finds room to flower, pushing through the dense layers of concentration. Must stay ahead now. No one to tell me how; I'm on my own. He stays right behind me. Oh lord. I lean more tightly over my tank; my neck aches from fatigue; my engine and the wind scream inside my helmet.

Rider ahead goes wildly down, went too high, caught the edge of the track. He is rolling across the track and away out of sight as I pass him, an object suddenly gone like scenery streaming past the window of a train I'm on. I feel neutral about his fall. I don't know who he was. I felt neutral about my own fall once, and I certainly knew who I was.

Oh beautiful for checkered flag! I sit up, slow down, ride an easy lap back to the pits. I think this is one of the most real things I've ever done. I've raced well, smoothly, not been last, not crashed. I ride into the pits, kill the engine, lean the beloved little white bike on a box, dismount, unzip my brown and white road-race leathers, let the jacket part flop down around my hips. My T-shirt is soaked with sweat. The wind and sun start to dry me off. I try not to swagger as I walk a little aimlessly, unwinding, feeling as if there is a glow all around me.

Then I grab my stopwatch and head for trackside to time laps for a friend in the next race. "Okay, Grace! Looked good out there!" a white-uniformed track official hollers at me as he hurries by. There's that feeling again, that sort of blossoming, as if I'm leaving flower petals behind me as I go, or a little trail of golden sparkles in the air.

Yes, thank you, and please, I *want* to look good out there. Like a real motorcycle racer. So far, so good. Motocross for three years on a Suzuki 125 — the ruts, the jumps, the mud, the foot-down turns; the jolting, slamming speed; the dust so dense I'm riding blind; the aching biceps and forearms and thighs; the wrenching around of my whole body. And now road racing, sinuous, graceful, the track a steady gray blur of speed, the little Yamaha 250 two-stroke shrieking beneath me as the tach climbs to the red line, reaching for the pavement with my knee in the turns.

Motorcycle racing in my forties. I've always liked going fast: running, horseback riding, driving on long, empty highways. On the street, on a motorcycle, going fast is not cool; it's too dangerous. But on the track the distance opens up into an endless horizon that I can speed toward as fast as I dare. I would call this ecstasy. I seek it out again and again.

After the checkered flag says I am through, I feel drained and exuberant, grateful to whatever turns of fate have led me to this track in this lifetime, grateful even for my name, which may be why I do these things. Funny, the way my name comes apart like that: Grace-race-ace. An echo. It tells me what to do, what to be. My parents named me Grace. I must have heard just "race."

"Okay," I said.